THE FUTURE OF
GERMAN DEMOCRACY

THE
FUTURE OF
GERMAN
DEMOCRACY

With an Essay "On Loss" by
GÜNTER GRASS

Edited by
ROBERT GERALD LIVINGSTON

and
VOLKMAR SANDER

CONTINUUM | NEW YORK

1993
The Continuum Publishing Company
370 Lexington Avenue, New York, NY 10017

Copyright © 1993 by The Continuum Publishing Company
"On Loss" by Günter Grass Copyright © 1992 by Steidl Verlag, Göttingen
under the title *Rede vom Verlust*

Printed in the United States of America

Library of Congress Cataloging-in-Publication Data

The Future of German democracy : with an essay "on loss" by Günter Grass /
edited by Robert Gerald Livingston and Volkmar Sander
   p.   cm.
  ISBN 0-8264-0597-5
  1. Germany—Politics and government—1990– 2. Democracy—Germany.
3. Germany—History—Unification, 1990. I. Grass, Günter, 1927–
  II. Livingston, Robert Gerald. III. Sander, Volkmar.
JN3972.A2F88 1993
943.087′9—dc20   93-2436
                                                   CIP

CONTENTS

PREFACE

ROBERT GERALD LIVINGSTON

Except for the United States, no country close to Germany welcomed its unification. Had France, Britain, and the Soviet Union been able to block or postpone unification they certainly would have done so.

Americans hardly noticed at the time that among many Germans, too, enthusiasm for unity was very faint. The Social Democrats' chancellor candidate spent his 1990 election campaign warning (all too accurately, as it turned out) about costs to come. The Greens of the time boasted that "everyone may be talking about Germany but we talk about the weather." Writers and intellectuals in western as well as eastern Germany were apprehensive. Like Günter Grass and others whose worries are set down in this volume or like the playwright Heiner Müller they were profoundly skeptical about unification from the start and opposed the shape that the unification process assumed after the spring of 1990.

Theirs were fears that had surfaced frequently over the previous forty years, strongly but by no means exclusively abroad,

and primarily but again not exclusively on the left: that unity of
the Germans must inevitably bring with it a rush of nationalist
feelings, a resurgent right, expansionism abroad, and repression
at home—an end, in short order, to the attachment to western
democracy, civic virtues, liberalism, and relative tolerance of
the *Bonner Republik*. Their dread has been—and remains—
that the "patriotism of the constitution" that a Jürgen Habermas had affirmed would give way to a Wilhelminian chauvinism that would sweep all along with it, including most likely
the intellectuals themselves.

For a few short weeks in early 1990, the left in the old Federal
Republic, ignored and politically impotent since Willy Brandt's
time two decades earlier, imagined an alliance with the democratic opposition that had come forth in East German communism's waning days, the Lutheran pastors, writers, feminists,
and democratic activists of "Democracy Now," "New Forum,"
and the "Initiative Peace and Human Rights." Such an alliance
of the left could, they dreamed, remake united Germany into
a far more just and social state than the old Federal Republic,
give it a better constitution, reform it broadly, preserve some of
the "social achievements" of the German Democratic Republic
(GDR), and renew the progressive spirit that had emerged in
1968 but had ended early in Brandt's chancellorship.

All too soon came the first free elections in the German
Democratic Republic, in March 1990. The East German voters
chose not social reform but the DM, not the SPD or New Forum
but Kohl and his Christian Democrats. The CDU interpreted
the mandate as immediate unification on terms set in Bonn and
total imposition of the institutions, norms, and values of those
who governed there.

Since then, as the essays in this volume testify, would-be re-
formers have seen many of their worst fears confirmed. Over
2,200 violent hate crimes against foreigners were recorded last

year—harrassment, beatings, firebombings, and murders—with the wave continuing undiminished into the spring of 1993. The "ugly German" reappeared in Hoyerswerda, Rostock, Mölln, and in hundreds of small towns in western as well as eastern Germany. Helsinki Watch, the American-based human rights organization, turned its attention to Germany for the first time, and its October 1992 report took the government and the police to task sharply for their delay, laxity, and thoughtlessness in dealing with acts of violence against foreigners.

And what of the great political fear—that a big, united Germany is turning rightward once again? Boehlich and Giordano seem convinced of it, Cohn-Bendit and Thierse less certain. In the dispirited East, alienated, bitter youths, most of them teenagers, have been rampaging in the streets, brandishing red-white-and-black nationalist banners, flinging up their right arms in the *Deutscher Gruss,* and howling for a "Germany for the Germans." In prosperous Bavaria, Baden-Württemberg, and Hesse Schönhuber and his *Republikaner* move up in the opinion polls and into local parliaments. Next time around they may well make it into the *Bundestag.* In their own clever, western way, the rightist parties also are exploiting German society's anxieties about the uncertainties, strangeness, and foreigners that unification has brought. Were the violent right in the East and the sophisticated right in the West ever to link and join behind an effective leader, then even some of the hysteria that occasionally emerges in these pages would turn out to be prescient and justified.

Brutal crimes by rightist punks and their flaunting of Nazilike insignia have been worrying officialdom and businessmen as well, as Heiner Geissler points out. Such displays, televised around the world, do damage to the new Germany's image abroad, frighten American Jews, and perhaps have cause foreign corporations to cancel investments in eastern Germany. It is entirely fitting, then, for the Foreign—not the Interior—Minister or Chancellor to pay the government's high-level visit to a concentration camp memorial torched by nightriders and to the Mölln apartment house where three Turks were firebombed to death by young rightists. (According to his spokesman, the Chancellor does not undertake that sort of "compassionate tourism.")

Much more is at stake in the civil republic today than its good name abroad, cries out Lea Rosch in this book. At stake are human rights, democracy, and the republic itself. Germany is on its way to new barbarism, Grass and Giordano insist.

One need not be blind to the new criminal brutalities in Germany or discount them or admit to liberal American naivité to insist in return that such predictions are overdrawn. Let me be clear: I do not myself believe that Germany is a fair weather democracy. The old Federal Republic faced economic strains, political tensions, and militant terrorism in the late 1960s and early 1970s. It surmounted its trials then, strengthened in its democratic spirit and institutions. It will surmount them again, if present indications are right.

In the months since the essays that follow were written, candle-carrying Germans by the millions have forged their "chains of lights" in Berlin, Munich, Hamburg, and dozens of other cities across the country. Slow and lax as it surely was at first to face up to violence on the right and to deal with it as effectively as it once had dealt with terrorists on the left, the government has now moved toughly against neo-Nazi groupings. Its backbone stiffened by the public demonstrations against xenophobia, it has trained the police to act against rightist criminality and has rapidly brought firebombers to trial.

Gingerly, hesitatingly, and of course opportunistically the parliamentarians have begun to wrestle with the complexities of amending the political asylum provisions of the constitution, developing an immigration policy and eventually legislation, and—hardest of all—reconsidering Germany's *völkisch* citizenship law.

It will not be easy. These are issues that go to the core of Germanness. They involve Germans' view of their own society, of their own worth to themselves, and to the world outside. Dealing with them will require changes of life-styles and mindsets, and the development of greater openness and tolerance than characterized either Germany after the war.

Vanished are the verities, certainties, and stabilities that prevailed for four decades in both Germanys. Preserving that great postwar German good, social peace was difficult enough in those two homogeneous states. How much harder it will be in diversity and in the what Freimut Duve calls a "hurricane of change of norms and values."

As long as Germans themselves worry about the directions they are taking and as long as essays like these appear, an American, like the Frenchman Alfred Grosser in this volume, need not fear Germany, even though he may fear for the Germans: But only as long, too, as the apprehensions expressed in this volume do not give way to self-pity but engender a will to find solutions that will not only protect but empower all, Germans and non-Germans alike, living within the borders of this now unified, somewhat larger, potentially much more powerful, indubitably democratic, still much-feared German state.

FOREWORD TO
THE GERMAN EDITION

WILHELM VON STERNBURG

We were lucky. Whether or not we deserved this luck remains to be seen. On May 8, 1945, the Allies freed us from the nightmare of a barbaric dictatorship and freed Europe from the yoke of the Germans. It took time for us to come to accept democracy as the most civil form of societal coexistence. This acceptance was not entirely voluntary, but was brought about through pressure—rather uncomfortable pressure at times—exerted by our Anglo-Saxon occupiers. The Germans east of the Elbe had a considerably more difficult time of it: they changed their ideological stripes and retained the dictatorship. They had to wait forty-four years for their moment of fortune. The revolution of autumn, 1989, which triumphed on the streets of Leipzig, Dresden, or Berlin, was an uprising that was quickly confronted with the irksome day-to-day tasks of material survival. And yet, it was—unlike the development in the first postwar years of West Germany—a "movement from below," which demanded and attained democracy and popular sovereignty. For the first time in the history of the Germans the revolution triumphed—the revolution, upon which in 1848 the majority had in vain staked its fortune, and which after 1918 had been so disgracefully betrayed by the elites in the administration, the military, and the courts. This mass uprising in the dying GDR was only able to remain "velvet," however, because "real existing Socialism" had filed for bankruptcy, and a political vacuum had emerged. The old order could no longer be upheld with bayonets.

Since the euphoric days of the Monday demonstrations and the breaches in the Berlin Wall, Germany has become not only larger, but colder as well. The politicians, who celebrated the regained unity with the pathos unique to them, proved themselves in an almost dramatic fashion to be incapable of reacting to the new challenges. Recognizing neither the mass psychological nor the economic dimensions of this epochal turning point, the governing Bonn administration relied as usual on administrative routine, when what was needed were conceptional creativity and sensitive empathy for the emotional and material condition of the new citizens of the Federal Republic. Thus began the big sellout in the East, and in the West indifference and selfishness grew.

This development is really not surprising. It began to manifest itself as early as the late 1970s, as the end of Marxism-Leninism was being discussed at most (if at all) in futuristic views and in prospects for the coming century. The shift to a new conservatism in Germany took place before the collapse of the Communist power structures in eastern Europe, and this shift was homemade. It took place during the years of the SPD-FDP coalition, as the economic-distribution struggles were becoming more heated, and debates over large-scale technical projects and gigantic NATO armament plans were increasingly dividing West German society into two camps. A generation emerged that reacted more and more sensitively to ecological destruction and the social hypocrisy of the elites. The pragmatism of politics, the dominance of materialism, the breaking apart of traditional social structures, the losses of authority becoming more and more apparent: all of these aroused frustration and fear about the future.

The consequences have long since become manifest. The cynicism of the affluent is met by the applause of those in power. The increasing brutality of the media is being reflected more and more in the social reality of our streets and schoolyards, and its echo can be heard in the chambers of our parliaments, in factory workshops, and in offices. Schools and universities atrophy in the shadows of the glass towers of banks and insurance companies; in nursing homes, death is organized coldly and pitilessly; society's tasks are being deliberately allowed to atrophy. Those unable to hold their own use drugs to create their own reality, only to end up in misery on one of the junkheaps of society. Germany—a civil republic?

Now they are screaming again, and murdering and pillaging as well. Houses are burning in Germany, Jewish cemeteries and concentration-camp memorial museums are being desecrated, and people are being chased through the streets because they are not German. The skinheads swing their bats, and the eternal narrow-minded petty bourgeois applauds. And the chancellor, incredibly, calls for a "state of emergency." In the Saxon town of Hoyerswerda the constitutional state shrank back visibly, for the first time, from the violence; since Rostock, this has become the German status quo.

History repeats itself: the role of the scapegoat, at one time assigned to the Jew, is now being forced upon the foreigner. The blame for adverse developments in our republic is being placed not on wrongheaded policies on housing, youth matters, social welfare, and finance, but on the "asylum seekers," the weakest members of this society. These are people who are seeking protection in the German state, protection from persecution, civil war, hunger, and distress. They are being confronted, however, with the modern barbarism that has ravaged this century time and time again, with "kill them all" arguments instead of tolerance, with violence instead of peace, with ideological con games instead of reason, with symbolic discussions of Article 16 of the Constitution and open threats by the CDU of a deliberate breach of constitution instead of humane application of existing laws. And the thugs are laughing up their sleeves; they have been bashing the democratic parties for quite some time now—today the Constitution, tomorrow the world.

It is no longer simply a matter of nipping the problem in the bud; we are already in the midst of it. German democracy is being threatened, since even this democracy can only have stability when it is defended by enough democrats. But the majority remains silent, and the minority, which is observing the burning torches on the German horizon with clandestine pleasure, is growing. For it is not the gangs of skinhead thugs who threaten the German republic, but rather the spirit, whose victims they have become. Right-wing extremism, nationalism, and racism are spreading again, like cancerous tumors, throughout Germany. The ideological wirepullers in their expensive suits have long since become respectable representatives of the German establishment, and their language has found its way into the political vocabulary of the democratic parties.

The chairman of the Central Council of Jews in Germany, Ignatz Bubis, whose right to call Germany his homeland was recently disputed by a CDU City Council member in Rostock, has in light of the recent desecration of the concentration-camp memorial museum in Sachsenhausen correctly pointed out that right-wing extremism is always anti-Semitic as well.

This thesis can quite easily be expanded: right-wing extremism was and always will be an opponent of civil democracy. Its postulates are violence and contempt for human rights. Its political programs do not offer rational proposals for the solutions to problems, but dogma.

The civil republic cannot be defended through appeals or books, but only through the conduct of its citizens. Not our words, but only our actions will have any influence on the social conduct of the up-and-coming generation—those who are now fifteen to twenty-five years old. Someone who on Sunday pledges his loyalty to the community but on Monday forces his political opponents out of the race with dirty tricks will never be able to convince anyone that decency and public spirit are virtues of our republic.

Expense-account scandals, constitutionally questionable party financing, dubious ties between the public and private sectors do not strengthen the republic, they weaken it. Corruption scandals within the ranks of the unions are just as damaging to the reputation of democracy as public servants who confuse their duty to the state with the interests of their party. The civil republic needs republicans with civil courage: politicians who know that they are independent representatives of the popular sovereignty, elected to limited terms of office, not parliamentarians-for-life in the service of the parties; clergymen who still have the courage to stand by the truth; parents and teachers who educate their children and pupils to be tolerant democrats and free people, not opportunistic conformists; trade unionists who look to the interests of their members and not their own personal power; journalists who think of their readers, listeners, and viewers, not their employers' pursuit of profit or their own careers. The list goes on and on.

Democracy without the constitutional state is unthinkable. Western parliamentarianism's liberal constitutions, whose origins are to be found in the American and French Revolutions of the eighteenth century, protect the citizen from the omnipotence of the state, but at the same time from the violence of his neighbor. The constitutional state is a foundation of the civil republic, but just as liberty must be defended each and every day, so also must justice, for without justice, liberty is lost. The basic rights in the Constitution of the Federal Republic of Germany begin with the sentence: "Human rights are inalienable." Whoever does not take this seriously has a hand in the destruction of the civil republic.

The editor wishes to thank the authors and Petra Eggers, the reader for Fischer Taschenbuch Verlag, for their contributions and their assistance. That the responses were so spontaneous, and that the necessity of such a book in light of the developments in our country has met with such broad-based consensus, can be taken as a sign of hope. Authors, political satirists and journalists, musicians, artists and actors, politicians, university professors, and theologians have all contributed to this book.

Translated by Martin Black

· 1 ·

GERMAN CONTINUITY

WALTER BOEHLICH

G ood living is living without moral taint. That being the case both individual and society will attempt to deny or relativize disgrace. Those caught and condemned make a few admissions in order to facilitate at least the appearance of a rehabilitation. This is coupled to brother confessor's obstinacy that he was not personally implicated in *everything* being pinned on him and by no means was it only all bad. At the very least his intentions, as well as the occasional act, were good.

The good that the Germans had wanted to do back then, from the first days of the Federal Republic on, back then in the early days of the disgrace, the disgrace that the majority, of course, did not perceive as such, was anticommunism. German democracy had scarcely broken stride in taking over this banner from the German dictatorship. The enemy was still leftist; he had stood his ground in the East. And since things were seen as such, in the eyes of Big Brother over the water as well, it was possible to convince oneself, consciously or unconsciously, that during the Nazi era one had stood at least half on the right side. As for the other half, it was more or less made up for by the fact that there was no longer any question that one now stood on the right side. The question that remained was one of how to integrate politically an overwhelming majority of formerly staunch and active Nazis into a state to which until only recently they had been utterly opposed. Obviously the easiest means to this was not to rob them of their nemesis—their disdain for leftists and hatred for the left—which could be so conveniently nurtured using the specter of so-called Communism with a capital C, i.e., socialism as it existed in the East. This resulted in a political landscape that silently suffered the poorly organized extreme right and adamantly opposed the radical left, both in society at large and in the political parties. Where leftists were to be found they were fenced out, especially in the FDP and the SPD—the two organizations that were not conservative by definition—but in the unions as well.

The Basic Law, a document whose original intention was supposedly that of making the return of the fascist right impossible and hence, at least within limits, understood itself as antifascist, transformed itself into one which essentially understood itself as anticommunist. In a prosperous welfare state the consensus deemed it possible to neglect the extreme right. More than mere belief, this in fact became practice. In contrast to the radical left with its terrorist enclaves the extreme right barely appeared in the reports of the internal intelligence community despite the fact that it existed both above and below ground.

But now the rightists have reemerged, are no longer underground, and, just as rightists have always done, they have stumbled upon all kinds of sympathy, not the least of which have been forthcoming in courts of law. We have been at pains to explain how misguided these poor chaps have been, embarrassed by them because of the memories of times long past they can potentially awaken around the world—why, even trade balances could be endangered—and yet we are helpless against them. We are helpless because we have ourselves fostered the conditions under which they have been able to flourish. Easing our consciences, we have ourselves ceased merely to flatter our egos that we are once again "somebody"; we have ourselves again yearned for a larger Germany; we have ourselves decided in favor of the thoughtless fetish for finally playing yet again under a new sign the international role to which, on the strength of our numbers and economic might, we Germans have been summoned.

A new generation has emerged for which all history appears to be prehistory, which possesses memories of neither inflation and dictatorship, nor war and true suffering, which feels overburdened by the smallest of recessions, by halfway tolerable cutbacks, by a future that has always appeared uncertain and rather dismal. This generation responds to social and political challenges by escaping into violence and irrationality. Rather than placing its faith in honest toil and reason, it turns to its Germanness and claims that the formula "Germany for the Germans" actually means something to them.

It may well be that history does not repeat itself, and yet, once again demands for a larger Germany have led to the most absurd chauvinism and most criminal acts of xenophobia. Surely not everyone has forgotten that the three wishes of fairy tales always come back to haunt the simpleton in the end. And this time? The first group sets hostels for asylum seekers ablaze, the second "flattens blacks," the third lays waste the remains of a concentration camp built by the master race, the fourth destroys Jewish cemeteries, the fifth awaits salvation while the wait-and-see partisans constituting the majority never tire of making assurances that right and left have now supposedly become obsolete concepts and are no longer of any use. Why?

Because this majority has spent a half-century preparing itself for nothing, neither for a potential confrontation with a rejuvenated right, nor for the political consequences of what was considered an unthinkable reunification, and least of all for the needs of the disenfranchised "third" of the "two-thirds society."

This majority has watched in silence as ever more wealth has been accumulated in ever fewer hands, and simply accepted as a matter of course that it is the little guy who gets stuck with the tab. Ultimately, they have effected what we call partisan peevishness that, in reality, serves as the best soil for antidemocratic messianism Neither a Western Connection nor an EEC will save us when an economic crisis emerges out of our present stagnation, when real unemployment can no longer be glossed over, when the costs of annexation prove unaffordable. We might at best be able to save ourselves—but that is something we have never managed to do.

Translated by Martin Black

· 2 ·

MULTI-CULTI; OR,
WHERE BARBARISM BEGINS

SILVIA BOVENSCHEN

Some people cannot suffer others. Normally, someone who is not readily suffered by another cannot himself suffer the first. It is difficult, but not impossible, to suffer someone you find insufferable. Most of the time, as long as the disinclination does not intensify to disgust, we do not find it all that insufferable when we cannot suffer somebody, and with advancing age we do a tolerable job of coming to terms with the fact that we are not ourselves always readily suffered by others. As long as we behave in a civilized fashion, even those whom we cannot suffer will not really have a great deal to suffer for. Etymologists, by the way, have pointed out that the German word for suffer [*leiden*], in the sense of "to be able to suffer someone," is not etymologically related to the German word for injury or harm [*Leid*]. The general associations with the word are not grief and pain, but rather that someone can more or less endure a situation, whether out of desire or necessity. As the bible has it: "[T]he day of the Lord is great and very terrible; who can endure it?" (Luke) [*sic*]*. And so we all know that we do not have much alternative but forever to endure it, just as we do the presence of our colleagues, relatives, and neighbors. It becomes more difficult when these aversions are directed at larger collectives—toward asylum seekers, for example, toward foreigners, strangers in general.

> One can't forever shun the foreign Mensch,
> Their merits, though, seem far away.
> Real German manhood cannot suffer much the French,
> Their wines, though, he'll drink any day.†

Would the boorish Brander from Auerbach's Cellar, into whose mouth Goethe placed the above words, still be tolerable for the project of multicultural appeasement? In the play *(Faust I)* Mephistopheles has some devilishly fiery fun with him. But this hellfire is harmless compared to what Brander would encounter were he to find himself plunked down unawares in our own times, engulfed by the moral barrage of invectives that such talk could elicite in many a locale. Let us assume for a moment that he landed among a group of multiculties, and uttered something to the effect that although he did not especially love Turks, he had a sweet tooth for Turkish honey.

Brander would immediately find himself furnished with a multiplicity of epithets, "chauvinist" being the tamest and most accurate, but there would certainly be no shortage of more extreme attributions such as "racist" and "fascist." A few of his foreigner-friendly interlocutors would recall—if only briefly to disburden themselves from forever doing good and being right—that they too at one time had flirted with the feeling that they could not tolerate the Japanese, for instance. The

---

*Actually Joel, 2:11, Revised Standard Version.
†J. W. von Goethe, *Faust 1*, 2270–73. Translation my own.

pragmatists among Brander's listeners might perhaps allow that
at least he was not a fanatic who scrupulously limited himself
to honey produced by German bees. "Resist the beginnings"
would be the response of the moralists, probably aware that
regular visits to an Italian restaurant is questionable proof of
openness to foreigners. On the other hand, the noble sushi bar
at which an Italian advertising executive celebrates the opening
of a multimedia business with a French designer and a German
cultural director is entirely safe: here one is insulated from
Kurdish drug dealers, from primitive nationalism, and from the
suspicion of xenophobia. It is the ideal locale for designing a
low-budget campaign against the hatred of foreigners. There is
actually quite a difference between placing one's children in the
safekeeping of an exclusive, international boarding school in
Switzerland, and sending them to a comprehensive school with
an extremely high percentage of foreign pupils where the cos-
mopolitan commandment of fraternity is radically challenged
by social, cultural, and religious multicultural conflicts. This
does not make it worse, but it definitely makes a difference.
Would Brander have the multisocial vision necessary to use
these considerations of milieu to immunize himself against the
multicultural suggestions of guilt? Probably not. This much,
however, occurs to him in his otherwise besotted brain: that
the ever-reproachful antifascist woman editor has little to do
with the irrational repercussions of the inequitable distribution
of wealth as she, ecologically correct wicker basket in hand,
ventures across the picturesque farmer's market, pausing to sate
her expensive pleasures not only with biodegradable products,
but with an exotic multiplicity of goods from all four corners
of the globe. Does Brander suspect, perhaps, that opposition to
racism and environmental consciousness are not solely, but can
be in part, a question of moral and economic affordability?
That these things are had more simply for some than for others?

Does the suspicion begin to grow in Brander that there are, as Heinrich Heine said, two types of rats—"those that are hungry and those well-fed," that the well-fed ones remain "content" at home while the hungry ones emigrate, and that this two-to-one proportion is forever stabilizing itself with the effect that the poor become poorer and the rich richer—and this not only locally in the microcosmic world of Auerbach's Cellar but on a worldwide scale? Does this specimen of "real German manhood" fear the loss of his miserable, petty unity; a unity he has been celebrating in the basement keep of his alcoholic stupor; its loss beneath the breaking wave of foreign poverty that threatens to drown this unity under a flood of new, multifaceted misery?

Is he only beset by fear and a plethora of aversions, or has he already made a small, yet decisive additional step? Has he already heard among the racist whisperings a particular pied piper, has he already woven together the divers threads of his diffuse aversions into the web of a political manifesto, and is he now prepared to find this politics of horror plausible because it corresponds so nicely to his unweeded inclinations? Has he jumped past the lip of civilization and does he now find himself not only unable to suffer those still hungry, but in fact hates them already, threatens them in the mad hope of being able to toss in his lot with that of the well-fed?

And yet, shocked as he is by the incomprehensibility of his living conditions, why in fact should Brander overburden himself with the commandment of brotherly love when he is simultaneously being offered nothing but simple, yet emotionally gratifying explanations for his unemployment, his need of an apartment, and his overall social misery? The guilty ones have been placed at his doorstep—the same ones that he is anyway unable to endure. And what offers have been tendered to counter demagoguery? No offers, just a commandment; the abstract commandment that one must be able to suffer all foreigners, all that is foreign. Those who have preached this for years have succeeded in turning a two-hour bus delay in Italy into an experience of un-German bliss. They too have gone one step further: their love for things foreign has been nurtured by their disdain for things close to home. Out of this aversion there grew a nationalism of guilt and responsibility, a negative nationalism against the backdrop of which one could dance with the impunity of being right and good. But Brander is not in a position to draw honey out of this blissful guilt. The conception that the entire immigration problem with a bit of goodwill and much moralizing could be turned into the good neighborliness of a town fair, this whole xenophile lullaby will not comfort him—in fact he may even catch the scent of dogmatism concealed from view. Above all, however, this kind of harmlessness contradicts his own experience.

Resist the beginnings of that into which the murder of asylum seekers and the howls of approval can develop! But where does it begin? Should we, can we deny our aversions? When we say about someone that we can suffer him well enough, we mean that we do not love him but can endure him well enough. When we say that we cannot suffer someone, we mean that although we do not hate him, we can joylessly endure him. We cannot suffer him, but we do not beat him to death. Thus civilization. The appeal that we should want to be able to suffer all foreigners or that we ought even to love them is absurd. None of us can follow such a call, not even in the cozy sphere of the cellar keep. It is difficult to discover the point at which an aversion turns into a passionate disposition, into a prejudice, a resentment, an ideological hatred. It is the point at which barbarism begins. Paradoxically, nothing seems to favor this shift more than the moralizing condemnation of every admitted aversion as vaunted barbarism itself.

Translated by Martin Black

·3·

THE BRUTAL REPUBLIC

DANIEL COHN-BENDIT

To get right to the point, I tend more toward the caste of the professional optimists, not that of the paranoid. Hence my conviction that not even the conservative majority of Social and Christian Democrats is prepared totally to place in question on the spur of the moment the laboriously acquired liberality and openness of this their republic. Of course the chancellor and the mayors of several Social Democratic cities will attempt to simulate a national state of emergency by stylizing the refugee migration as *the* problem facing the Federal Republic, but the debate concerning Article 16 of the Basic Law and the guarantee of basic rights laid down in Article 19 indicates that sufficient forces can be mobilized in order to organize an open discussion in this question. The openly manifested willingness in Rostock, Hoyerswerda, Hünxe and elsewhere to practice and affirm racist acts of violence has both frightened various social circles and, of course, mobilized a majority of politicians relevant to the decision-making process who nonetheless furtively hide behind these deeds.

I believe it would be unsophisticated simply to say that this republic has drifted to the right since unification. Phenomena of brutalization like those we have experienced in recent months characterize the condition of societal confusion in all western democracies. In times of an economic and moral crisis that all late capitalist societies are presently experiencing, this uncertainty expresses itself in an increasingly violent form. Brutalization by youths in soccer stadiums, on the street against foreigners and asylum seekers, brutalization in marriages and relationships in the form of child abuse and rape and, to cite yet another example, the increase in violent war games, not to mention a rise in pornographic, sadomasochistic mass fantasies. Following this line of thought, racism and anti-Semitism become an expression of the aforementioned social brutalization. It is for this reason that a reduction of the discussion around this social phenomenon to a simple matter of possibly changing an article of the constitution appears inadequate and dangerous. It appears as if morality, which for a long time now has served as the basis for consensus in our society, only applies to periods of pleasant prosperity. For when hopelessness and a lack of perspective go hand in hand with paranoid power and potency fantasies, when masculine fanaticism once again becomes a generally accepted social category, then the senseless debate on the constitution by rightists, social tinkerers, and moral apologists expresses rather a breach in social reality rather than the attempt intellectually to come to grips with this reality.

The brutalization that has articulated itself on the right, and the increase in fascination with it, demonstrates that a growing number of people are allowing themselves to be swayed by simple "solutions." We can either complain about this state of affairs or, as leftists and/or enlightened liberals, self-critically turn it to good use against ourselves, for it proves that we are apparently incapable of transforming the increasing complexity of social relations into politically stabilizing programs. The ongoing lamentation over the rightist reductionists and demagogues is of no use to anyone. Especially because the right has always had an easier time of representing apodictically egotistical positions as the legitimate preservation of national prosperity, the political vision of a humanitarian position is required here, not group therapy sessions at leftist tea parties for coping with this imminent disaster. This republic brutalizes itself on the right and elsewhere because, following the collapse of socialism as it existed in the East, the emancipatory alternatives often wedge themselves too tightly to the grooves of their traditional thinking. Here is an indication of how difficult it will be to climb out of this vale of tears. For we must be prepared to dispense publicly with our own historical mistakes and at the same time define anew from these present ruins the right and proper appeals for equality and solidarity. Citing the conservative camp for its inability self-critically to appraise its own history will not help us; it is exactly this that is supposed to differentiate the left from the right—namely its ability to confront its own history, its own position, and publicly debate mistakes and errors.

The reaction of the republic to the problem of the increasing numbers of asylum applicants is an expression of how unstable the democratic and collective achievements of our society actually are. It would nonetheless be wrong, with the consciousness of our marginal status, to take once again the moral high road, apodictically postulating responses for our own sake without first considering their chances for implementation. At this point in European history it is necessary that minimal civilizing criteria be maintained or implemented.

For this reason we will have to wrestle our way through the difficult process of political debate toward a historic compromise concerning issues of immigration and asylum. This compromise will then serve as the yardstick for the measure of this society's civilizing disposition. Only when we have succeeded in inscribing into the constitution civil rights for immigrants and asylum seekers already here, in rooting out of the constitution every racial and ethnic definition of the nation, in simultaneously securing real and generous protection for political refugees, only then will we all emerge, unmolested and at least partially upstanding, from this brutalizing social confrontation. I would caution the left against entrenching itself in the rhetoric of dogmatic righteousness, seeking to be proven right by future historians, allowing in reality for defeat in order to ascertain smugly in the end that this republic has once again slid to the right.

If we find ourselves unable to strike a compromise with the popular majority in which our proposals and alternatives are taken into consideration, then this will once again be an expression of the chronic political impotence from which we on the left suffer. I, for one, do not care to be proven right by future historians. I want rather to do what I can to prevent people's fears, which exist here and now in this society, from being used to legitimize the actions of a conservatively positioned social order. The brutal republic is not a necessary, but rather a possible development. As an alternative we posit a just and collective democracy.

Translated by Martin Black

· 4 ·

BLOWS FROM OFFSTAGE—
AN ADMONITION TO CONCRETION

FRIEDRICH DIECKMANN

1

"Voices against the right" are supposed to be gathered here; this, in fact, was the working title of this collection. It sounds plausible, but what does it mean? Is it actually voices we are dealing with when we consider the "right wing" (wherever this may be)? Or is it perhaps only thugs? The dramatist Jochen Berg was telling me about a visit he made to a pub not far from his apartment in the north of downtown Berlin, a crumbling, run-down area, but before the monetary union a thoroughly untroubled one. Several young men enter, casting threatening glances about; he tries to defuse the situation with a few lighthearted words spoken to one of the young men, and before he knows it, he receives a punch in the face that sends him reeling. A few days earlier I had read in a Berlin daily newspaper, *Der Tagesspiegel*, about a reporter who made an excursion to a disco on the outskirts

of the East German town of Hoyerswerda. The young reporter
wanted to have a look at this rendezvous of the local youth;
he entered the public establishment—and barely managed to
escape a gang, who without warning, without even a preliminary dispute, punched his teeth in. In the last second he managed to jump into his car, which his female companion, sensing
danger, had already started. The policeman to whom he reported the incident asked him insistently if he had in any way
provoked the attack. When he denied this, he was informed
that his large stature must have had a provocative effect.

Cut to the center of the center, to the intersection of Fried-
richstrasse and Unter den Linden, the main crossroads of downtown Berlin. A man in a smart blue coat and white collar, with
a friendly, polite face, is leaning in the doorway of a new pub.
He extends his hand toward the person approaching, the index
and middle fingers raised in an ostentatious "V." As I pass by,
I ask him, "Who is the victory sign for?" "For Germany!" he
slurs cheerfully. A businessman celebrating the fact that he has
just pulled off a successful *Treuhand* deal? Perhaps he has run
an immense risk with his investment in the East and is now
seeking reassurance in his patriotism. A voice from the right?

Voices *against* the right—this would only make sense if there
were voices *from* the right. There has been a quite constant
stream of such voices in the Federal Republic from its very
beginnings. For decades, nationalistic sectarians have been ral-
lying around such newspapers as the *National-Zeitung*. I
bought such a paper last year at a newsstand in Leipzig; among
the topics covered were the reclaiming of Northeast Prussia*
and the contradiction inherent in the circumstance that a country with such a strikingly low birthrate as Western Germany
spends so much more money on sheltering and feeding for-

---

*Territories that now belong to Poland and Russia.

eigners than on "protection of motherhood" and promotion of the family in Germany.

That was a voice from the right; a mixture of sheer demagogy and real problems. To elude the demagogy would be futile, if one did not at the same time address the conflict potential that constitutes its driving force. One of the strengths of the GDR was its highly developed system of programs for the protection of the welfare of mothers. This system, which naturally operated at the expense and to the detriment of the production operations, consisted of a comprehensive network of day-care facilities and nursery schools. Cutbacks are planned (or have already been carried out), working mothers are worse off than ever; they are being affected by the rising unemployment to an overproportionate extent. The birthrate in the former East Germany is now lower than in West Germany; some sources report a drop of 50 percent. There can be no clearer indication of the condition of a country so adversely affected by the bankruptcy of its own system and by the predominance of a system imposed from without. The gynecological clinics in the former GDR hospitals are filled with women undergoing sterilization operations; a child would be a threat to any potentially attainable job. What are the political implications of such behavior?

In Berlin and in West German cities, I do not see the *National-Zeitung* for sale on the newsstands, and I wonder which is better: to try and gain insight into this world of thought, which is actually a world without thought, and to find out which real problems are being referred to by the pithy verbiage, or to perceive only the violence. It is important to have a look at these papers. And it is fortunate that this is usually not easy to do.

But do the thugs and rowdies actually fill their heads with newspaper articles? Are the thugs the physical extension of the headlines in the *National-Zeitung*? To presuppose this would be to infer that there is indeed a thought behind the deed—this, however, would be an inadmissable intellectual shortcut. Voices from the right—they have accompanied four decades of development in the Federal Republic of Germany, in the form of newspapers and clubs, of expellee associations and *Waffen-SS* clubs operating under the surface of an indignant public. But to diagnose that this seed has suddenly and violently sprouted would be hasty. The aggression is the primary phenomenon here; we are not dealing with voices, but with the opposite of voices. We are dealing with a form of violence that opposes all articulate thought; it would for this reason be careless to label it "right wing" for the sake of the reassurance offered by rational categorization. It would constitute an abstract reaction to concrete dangers.

These dangers express themselves in many different ways. Are those undecipherable symbols that have been appearing ever since the monetary union on the walls of East German cities signals from the right? These warning signs of a civilization, whose progress we now share with the western part of the nation, look from a distance like Chinese characters. But they are shapeless; to express nothing is their very meaning—signals from a world beyond the realm of written language, and directed against it. They are anticharacters, the menacing harbingers of a postalphabetical, postcultural agglomeration that appears to be on the verge of wanting to take the place of society. These symbols constitute precise retorts to those gigantic billboards on legally sanctioned walls, which with colorful pictures and alluring slogans indoctrinate us with the glitter of the world of consumer goods. They are emanations of a loss of meaning that duplicates itself in chaotic scribblings. Political catchwords and product advertising had long since disappeared from the billboards of the GDR, on which then appeared almost exclusively announcements for concerts, plays, and exhibitions. Their sudden return constituted a culture shock.

I found a bit of graffiti that was not only decipherable, but witty as well, on the wall of a house in the Kreuzberg district of West Berlin. It was most likely written there when West Berlin was still an island; it read: "A lion for every Christian." But that is no solution either. Was it a voice *from* the right or a voice *against* the right?

The menacing harbingers of a postalphabetical agglomeration—already I find myself in the trap of substitution, which presumes intentions and goals, when it is the very absence of these that constitutes the nature of the phenomenon. This abomination does not symbolize a claim to power over society. It is a call for help *within* society. There are two gestures used by those who feel themselves forced to the margins of society; they differ in respect to the activities they symbolize. One is the outstretched hand, the upturned hat of the alcoholic with the furrowed face and the knowing, desolate eyes, the empty stare of the twelve-year-old accordion player on the concrete plaza in front of the train station—the pleading, humble gesture of the outsiders, the lost. The other gesture is the resounding blow to the face of those who try to establish through language a relationship, which because of the circumstances can in the end only be fictitious, i.e., patronizing, not because those who want to speak lack goodwill, but because they are unable to understand the situation truly.

The reporter who visits the local pub of those who draw attention to themselves with their fists—because they do not want to draw attention to themselves by begging—represents through his mere presence a provocation, like the Russian grand duke who, undisguised, makes a personal inspection of the exile camp: the punch in the face ends the scouting-out mission. It brings the group together again; they recognize their common bond in the act of aggression, and identify themselves with it. Defining themselves through attack, they reject the passive perspective that opens itself to those rejected and overtaxed by society: drugs, alcohol, prostitution. The punch in the face of the other transcends the drug, it is the remedy against booze, hashish, cocaine. The puncher does not care whether his blow strikes a bum, an intellectual, or a policeman; all that matters is that his reaction is an active one.

For if one were to behave passively, then drugs would be the final stage. But those who behave actively find no other means, within or without, then the cudgel, the Molotov cocktail, or the switchblade. Drugs and weapons are already circulating freely in schools, not only North American schools, which are equipping themselves like high-security tracts without affording any security. This only appears to be a marginal phenomenon. It is in reality a matter that affects the very foundation: society.

2

Leaving the one world and entering the other, we experienced this culture shock as well, an even greater one: the skinhead thug *and* the wretched beggar; we experienced them as two sides of a new world. Of course, skinheads did exist in the old world as well. They set the tone in the football stadiums; the ubiquitous "bureau of destabilization" would deploy them against oppositional groups: good squads used as a cudgel against environmental groups. Even in GDR days these young men, who had never seen a Jew, were quick to express anti-Semitic sentiments. But whoever tried to expose this activity for what it was, in verse or in prose, came up against brick walls. This bankruptcy, too, was hushed up with taboos. Poor people existed, and alcoholics; who knows how many of them would have stood on the street with an upturned hat if they had not been certain of being picked up by the police. Still, there were no homeless; food, clothing, and shelter were always provided, inadequate as they may have been at times; the absence of drugs was provided for as well. And ex-convicts were given jobs, even when they were quite incompetent; they held the coal delivery monopoly tightly in their dissolute hands. The patriarchal state set store by security, not only in regard to police work. And the police, who would have registered and sent on his way any street beggar they came across, also kept the violent criminals in check, whose groups, like other groups as well, they had infiltrated. They did not prevent everything, but by no means did they prevent only the worst.

Those bodies responsible for keeping order were effective not only through their capability of action; their mere presence absorbed energies. Those all too willing to perpetrate violence had in them an adequate opponent, whose presence kept the potential for aggression in check. This all belongs to the past. The state as opponent has disappeared, driven out of power by the collective rage of the people, drowned in financial power. But this financial power works in a diffuse manner, and has no structuring effect. The vestigal police have had the nightsticks, which they hardly ever had to use, wrested out of their hands; they have fallen into discredit as an organ of the dictatorship, not least in their own eyes. But the new judges from the affluent areas hand down sentences of only a few weeks in jail for serious disturbances of the public peace, and these sentences have generally been served with the time the defendants spent in pretrial incarceration.

The violence-prone young people have lost their opponents, which makes them intoxicated; they have lost their jobs, which makes them bitter. They have been aware of the powerlessness of their old opponents since 1989, when the citizens' movement proved itself unwilling as well as incapable of filling the power vacuum left behind by the bankrupt SED, and from December on, they set the mood for the Saxon demonstrations, the Monday demonstrations in Leipzig. Then came the new power with its altogether different types of levers—a coercive force that, unlike the old one, was not addressable, but that rather as an economic (and consequently impersonal) pressure was able to elude all attempts to counter it. The political and medial Western powers, who initiated the process with incredible carelessness and stupendous ignorance, should have known what that meant. But they were not living in the present. In a mixture of bravado and consternation, they had removed themselves to a completely different time from the present; they dug up old, long-buried hatchets and fought diligently in abandoned trenches. The only way they were able to come to terms with their terrible victory was to not believe in it, and to act as though they had to defeat once again their vanquished opponent, as the phantom of a Trojan horse.

That was, in all civility, a curious transposition of the old Stalin model, which had consisted in constantly producing anew in a fictitious form the "enemy of the working class," which had not only been conquered, but which had disappeared altogether; just so as not to have to face reality. Completely occupied with ousting a system that had just ousted itself, and without a thought to the requirements of a completely new situation, a large back door was opened to the clumsy, but, as it soon proved itself, highly effective rhetorical strategy of those who had even in the old, iron world felt themselves to be outsiders. These people could now enjoy the feeling of becoming representative; representative for a population, who through the dizzyingly abrupt changes in the conditions of their existence, through the deep destabilization of all the forms of their existence, felt themselves to have been made foreigners in their own country. In those poorer people, who had been brought by human smugglers from the Transylvanian mountains to this crisis-ridden country, and who had been placed in front of their noses by the thoughtless, if not cynical authorities imported from West Germany, they may well have seen the image of what they would become if they did not dance to the tune of the free-market economy: pariahs of an underdevelopment they themselves are being persistently blamed for by the new order.

3

That the consternation is making itself felt in the West as well, where its origins go back further, is evident. If it seemed to the East Germans, yearn as they might to be a part of the world of hard currency, as though they had suddenly been made foreigners in their own country, the West Germans began to feel as though they had been burdened with sixteen million more mouths to feed: the citizens of the former GDR, who, although according to the laws of the Federal Republic of Germany were considered to be fellow citizens, since according to these very laws the GDR was seen as nothing more than a territory of the Federal Republic, were perceived as foreigners, as "German-speaking Poles." The majority of the West Germans do not perceive them this way, but an exasperated minority does. And a government and an opposition who had had any imagination should have known that the German unification would have to exacerbate the foreigner problem, which had long since reached critical proportions in the old Federal Republic, not because of any moral deterioration, but simply for statistical, practical, and psychological reasons. And that is how it happened, while the politicians and statesmen were busy exchanging points of view that were being made obsolete by reality on a daily basis. This process, running on two separate tracks (for in the East, a problem was abruptly created that had been present in the

West for quite some time), was just as foreseeable as the collapse of the East German economy. The result is nevertheless
surprising: opinion polls as well as elections indicate that what
expresses itself as xenophobia but what in reality is something
much simpler—the misplaced demand for what is perceived by
many to be inadequate public relief—that this attitude is en-
countered to a much greater extent in the affluent West than
in the poor East, which is being swept into an expropriation
process, of which the West Germans have a vaguer notion than
of the billions of marks being transferred.

The East, for all the security it is being afforded by such a
highly developed social welfare state, is being swept into this
expropriation process to such a dramatic extent, that what is
astounding are not the outbreaks of violence the newspapers
are reporting on in areas where a doubly reckless economic
policy, that of the old and the new central authority, has all
but killed off industry and agriculture, as well as the clubs and
activity centers once connected with the factories and agricul-
tural collectives, but that the riots are remaining isolated and
localized, and showing no signs of growing into a widespread
conflagration. The extraordinary discipline and clearheaded-
ness of a population that through constant education by circumstances and by their leaders had been taught to accept the
inevitable, and that again feels called upon to do so, as well
as the safety net of social welfare benefits accompanying an
economic process that amounts to a gift-wrapped coloniza-
tion—these factors bring about, for all the isolated horrors, an
overall image of tranquillity. West German politicians who have
ventured into the new territories of the former GDR and who
are responsibly engaged in their rebuilding, never fail to imagine
how the West German population would react if they were to
find themselves in a similar situation.

Yet, the clear failure of the Diestel-Gysi Justice Committee has to arouse suspicion. It means that the population recognizes even this PDS-affiliated initiative as one of those varieties of protest, of proven ineffectiveness, which the pluralistic system provides in great number. Apparently these committees, which are decried as cover organizations of the Communists, are like the parties seen as system-immanent instruments for the consequence-free purgation of painful social emotions. Thus, the failure of these committees is more disquieting than their success would have been. This failure seems to indicate that the real protest will not take on a left-wing character, nor will it manifest itself in the form of committees.

The transitional subsidies afforded to the new territories are running out; a "solidarity tax," now more necessary than ever, is being unceremoniously dropped (for the unification strategists' idea that the new economy in the former GDR would start pulling its own weight as well of that of the state apparatus within three years is revealing itself to be what it always was: an illusion); other types of subsidies, at the level of the *Bundesländer,* for example, are being hotly contested. The GDR was created in the West German image, but its troubles are still being treated as though they belonged to a foreign territory, not one's own; now the West is even further away from being able, from the consciousness of the whole, to mobilize the actions of the whole. This constitutes an irresponsible risking of the unthinkable: the reinstatement of double statehood. This would not be a nonviolent process, as was the abolition of the double statehood in 1990. All those backward-looking blood brothers and friends of the German apocalypse aesthetic who have recently been complaining that a political upheaval could take place so peacefully and without bloodshed, an upheaval that would have released energy and kept the old government in power, would have something to gloat about. For such a reversion back to double statehood would take the form of an eruption of violence that at first merely breaks out sporadically and symptomatically. One thing is certain: such an outbreak would not take place under left-wing auspices. Such an out-break would send the helpful, crafty Manfred Stolpe, the eloquent Marianne Birthler, and the untiring Ulf Fink, it would send Christa Wolf and Frank Schirrmacher, Hans Modrow, Wolf Biermann, and many others into one of those deserts that are suited perfectly for the revision of history.

4

Voices against the right? It would be a mistake to assume that the political spectrum lies on a straight line. It has the form of an open circle, and the detonations always take place when a spark jumps across the gap between left and right at the extreme ends. Meanwhile, blows are coming from offstage, and sometimes we hear voices, but do we actually perceive them as well? We hear the voice of the singer-hero, who murders in effigy by blacking out the photographs of various people, to whom three years ago, as they still managed to hold on to a bit of power, he either showed kindness or paid respect, and publishes such blacked-out photographs by the millions. He does with words and images what those less conversant with the use of words and images try to do with their fists to people with other disadvantages. He, too, is being consumed by the great emptiness left behind by the vanished opponent. And he, too, babbles at the end of his attack that he did not really mean it that way, and that he only wanted, in his stupid rage, to let off steam.

The verbal drama of ego-intoxicated helplessness—that, too, is a symptom; other voices are to be taken more seriously. The Magazine *Stern* listens to a sixteen-year-old girl's depiction of the state of mind of those who see nothing wrong with setting fire to refugee shelters; her boyfriend is in jail—not only did he storm the shelter, but the police cordon as well. It becomes apparent (as one could well have guessed) that what we are dealing with here are abandoned children—abandoned by their parents, whom the new times, the undreamt-of troubles have caused to drift apart; abandoned by any prospects for meaningful work; abandoned by the demands, once belittled and now sorely missed, placed on them by the "security state": "I used to be in the Young Pioneers. We did garden work in the schoolyard in the afternoon. And later, in the Free German Youth, we'd clean up streets and parks. Back then, I thought the whole thing was pretty stupid. But now, I really miss it sometimes. It was nice to have somebody tell you you were doing a good job once in a while."

They are abandoned people, who express themselves only too well: "It's like, none of you in the West can understand, it's totally dead here, nothing ever happens. You have to make something happen yourself. How life *could* be, you only see on TV. Or if we go to Hamburg or Berlin. What it all comes down to is money, and we don't have any. We'll probably never have any. I have this dream, where I'm riding a horse along the beach. Not here. In California or somewhere. Right into the sunset. Kind of a bullshit dream, huh?"

A voice from the right? Or a voice from the left? "Then I picked up my Ringo at the animal shelter," continues the six-teen-year old, whose aunt did not want to give her the kitten (she would rather have killed it), "He was the scrawniest one there. He was crouching all the way in the back of the cage and shivering. I petted him, and said to him: Well, it looks like you don't have anybody either. So come on. Nah, I don't like people anymore. And they don't give a shit about me, either—except for Toddy."

Toddy, her boyfriend (the one who stormed the refugee shel-ter, and who is now in jail), as it turns out, actually does read the *National-Zeitung;* he has also been to conventions of the

Deutsche Volks-Union. "It's better than getting into trouble with his buddies." The right-wing party as an organization that fills the vacuum society and the state have created by tolerating it; right-wing extremism as the active form of social welfare. From the head to the arm is not the direction of disaster, but the other way around; someone who is trying to drown out emptiness with violence is searching for something that looks like a handhold. One entertains oneself by stealing cars, and soon masters the art so well, so excessively, (and unmolested as well, due to the hopeless inadequacy of the police), that it becomes boring. Storming the refugee shelter is a lot more exciting, the provocation is taken up, the state makes a conspicuous, albeit weak and belated, appearance—and already one has two opponents. In front of the burning shelter, then, stands the man from the DVU, he himself unemployed, and hands out copies of the *National-Zeitung.*

It is not the case of the wrong theory being transformed into concrete violence. Violence, rather, which comes about as a protective reaction to the great emptiness, finds something that looks like a thought. If nothing else can give one self-esteem, the knowledge that one is a German will have to do. And people hold on to this pride in being German all the more tightly, the more those in the media, those with a public voice (a voice, by the way, denied to most of the "proud to be a German" crowd) declare their Germanness to be not a good, but an evil, a questionable, anything but distinguishing quality, something that lessens, not strengthens their self-esteem. Here, too, is a gaping vacuum, which has been created with no little effort. Stale air rushes in with a hiss. Dragon's teeth grow only on fallow fields.

5

That which in the East is appearing in the wake of an abrupt shock to people's sense of security in all areas of life, the syndrome of aggressive fear of people who are different, who are seen as the drop that causes the barrel of one's own insecurity to overflow; this syndrome appears in the West as the result of an asylum-granting policy that to a large extent was something quite different—an immigration policy left to its own devices. The statistics speak for themselves; it turns out (*Fischer World Almanac 1992,* Columns 319, 346) that in early 1990, approximately 190,000 foreigners, a little less than a third of which were Vietnamese "guest workers," lived in East Germany; this represents 1.12 percent of the population (they lived in peace and unmolested). Furthermore, 343,854 emigrants from East Germany, 377,055 ethnic German emigrants from Eastern Europe, and a surplus of 330,000 immigrants (i.e., the number of immigrants minus the number of emigrants) from other countries moved to the old Federal Republic in 1989. That makes a total of 1,050,909 new inhabitants within the space of one year, or 1.67 percent of the total population, a population that in 1988 included 7.7 percent foreigners; more than twice as many as in the old colonial power Great Britain (3.1 percent), and much more than in France as well (5.8 percent), where, unlike in Germany, a formidable right-wing party already exists. *Numeri terrent.* These numbers signalize an overload; skeptical observers are interpreting them in such a way as to suggest that certain responsible parties *want* to stir up a crisis, a crisis that could only erupt towards the right. To read intentions into this deplorable state of affairs would be thoughtless; what we are seeing is the inability to come to terms with these empirically deplorable conditions through political action. Is it a systematic inability? We previously held the incapacity for feedback to be the hallmark of monocentric systems.

The overload is articulating itself quite directly. A taxi driver from the West Berlin district of Wilmersdorf, a young man of about thirty-five, talks about Brokdorf and the enormous mobilization of police troops sent there to protect the atomic plant (which has since been shut down) from left-wing protesters. He compares this with the minimal police protection afforded to refugee shelters when the need arises. As we drive through Kreuzberg, he tells me about school classes, in which hardly one-fifth of the pupils are German. If *his* family lived in such a neighborhood, he would have to move away from Berlin, since the instruction in such classes would necessarily take place at the expense of those who already speak German: the Germans. A voice from the right?

Various causes are thus evident. Yet to name these causes could lead to the suspicion that, by explaining something, one is justifying it. Such defensive positions are a preliminary stage of totalitarian thinking. To take circumstances and contexts into account strikes them as suspicious; only emotional reactions to isolated phenomena satisfy the strictest standards. But even that is understandable. For if one did not detest casually approaching the phenomena of terror, one would have to draw conclusions. One would have to stop mirroring oneself through one's own speech; one would have to face reality. But that is painful; it is much easier to moralize.

I hear, from various directions, that one should empathize not with the perpetrators, but with the victims. This exhortation is a variation of that defense that exists helplessly on the surface of things. It is imperative to be acquainted with the positions, the motives, the spheres of experience, and the emotional states of potential and virulent perpetrators of violence; one needs this knowledge to be able to deal with the acts of violence. The potential and the real victims do not need empathy, they need protection. This protection must manifest itself on all levels. It must, in the face of threats, take the form of effective police protection; this requires an investment of money and ideas. It has been exactly two years since the new state gathered police troops from distant areas of West Germany and sent them to Mainzer Strasse in East Berlin to drive out a few left-wing squatters. At that time, armored vehicles of the Federal Border Patrol were lined up on Alexanderplatz; it was the first time such pieces of equipment had ever been seen there. Where were they in Rostock or Hoyerswerda?

A technically, politically, and psychologically functional police force needs to be set up in the five new Federal States, not only to protect the foreigners from the natives, but to protect the natives from themselves as well—on the streets of these suddenly overmotorized areas. Here the number of people killed runs into the hundreds; children included—they are all victims of an aggressive absence of reason and of a lack of adequate state control; victims of a unification process that has been left partly to its own devices, partly to the vagaries of resentment. It is furthermore a matter of legal positions and judicial authorities; if one only has to serve a few weeks in jail for a serious breach of the public peace, then incarcerations will not improve anything.

Extending the powers that quell violence and that bring its perpetrators to justice is nevertheless but *one* form of necessary protection, one aimed at the symptoms, not the causes. A more far-reaching extension of these powers must needs promote the integration of those who, coming from distant lands, find it all too easy to enter this country, but who have all too difficult a time of it finding acceptance here. The catchword "multicultural society" is one of those well-meaning concepts that obscure the nature and the extent of the problems rather than shed light on them. For these concepts presuppose, as it were, this prerogative of the educated classes called culture, and give the impression that it was a matter of the immigrants' being able to establish their own churches and read books in their own language. But this is not where the root of the problem lies. The problems arise when the right to asylum, robbed of all substance not by incorrect wording but by wrongheaded practice, is made into an open floodgate for unregulated immigration. Of the 771,000 foreign immigrants in 1989, only 121,300, or 15.7 percent, were asylum seekers (according to the 1992 *Fischer Almanac*, p. 319).

It is important that those who have come to our country retain their own culture; for their new existence in a new country it is above all important that they learn the language of their host country and acquaint themselves with *its* culture. For both of these are prerequisites for gaining a foothold in their professional lives. If the measure of acceptance does not orient itself to the possibility of real integration, in economic as well as in civic life, an army of uprooted people will be created, which stands (that is, between its native and adopted languages and cultures) truly at home nowhere, a subproletariat beneath the subproletariat. Its creation can only bring about one thing: the production of a terrorist climate at the foundations of society, a climate that would keep the whole of society in a state of fear and terror, and that in an anarchistic or mafialike fashion would outdo what the secret police forces of the now defunct Socialism brought about by bureaucratic means. To the children of the third millennium, the actions of the Stasi would then look like child's play.

Translated by Daniel Theisen

·5·

IN THE HURRICANE OF CHANGE

FREIMUT DUVE

Since Rostock one thing that has received short shrift concerns the deeply seated, creeping psychic fear shared by millions of citizens about whom it is supposed from their appearance that their grandparents were not German. They may well have lived here for thirty years, or been born here, but the fear has nonetheless gripped many by the throat. They are aware that they have in this country potential assailants who might beat them to death, that there are thousands willing to aid the assailants, thousands unwilling to aid the victims. We are dealing here with the terror of cold-blooded murder.

Terror of expulsion. The tawdry dream that we Germans have once again become what we never were in our history: a culturally and racially homogeneous people. Only now is the fall of the Wall truly resulting in culture shock, only now are people truly realizing what kind of immigration "free" anomaly the Federal Republic has developed into over the past forty years by having its door to the East boarded up.

Throwing Wide the Gate

Throwing wide the gate. The old phrase *Tür und Tor* precisely designates the source of our fears. Ours is a culture of lockable doors. They have apparently made a greater impression on us than have religion or politics. Our doors are the kind that, secure on their hinges in a door frame, can be unlocked but also locked. To have a home means to exercise at any time the right of access to the front door, to open or close the door, to receive guests, to let strangers in or not to let them in. Medieval cities regulated rather precisely security of gate control. Cultures lacking doors and gates create a different kind of precise system for determining who belongs and who does not. I recall my own shy timidity when, in the early sixties, I visited Mashona Dörfler to interview her for a scientific paper. None of the huts had doors, but I waited until I was asked by someone at the entrance of her hut to state my business. The respect for borders, gateless ones as well, is a part of all cultural life. The opposite of this is war: violent invasion or attack. In Central Europe this was most recently done by German soldiers: attack across the border, invasion of cities and homes. Protection against this is insured by Article 13 of our Basic Law according to which no one is allowed in, nor can intrude with audio or visual surveillance, and least of all the state.

Just as we perceive our homes, and this includes us open and liberal intellectuals as well, so too our perception of our state: we frequently leave the door wide open, but we can, when the wind blows, shut it tight again. In reality, however, no democratically constituted state has at its disposal an entranceway that always functions as do the doors to our homes.

And yet this is exactly what we expect deep down. Hence the dilemma of the immigration and asylum debate: the duty of granting shelter versus the fear of an unlockable door. Article 16 is increasingly perceived as the adversary of Article 13—as a housekey for all those who want in and against whom not even the door chain is of any use. That is the dilemma of the politics in this debate. It is faced with representing the constitutional and social state of the German Federal Republic as a precisely defined house in which everything is running fairly well and whose doors are occasionally open, but also frequently shut. And at the same time we (politicians) are constantly faced with the task of adjusting this skewed image. For, in a society of eighty million in the middle of Europe with long borders shared by neighboring countries, none of which can any longer be considered police states, this society is only marginally capable of good door policy. Anyone propagating the illusion that it is possible to install door and gate and then shut them is deceiving the voters.

But back to our own homes. The closed door is a signal of security for the inhabitants of the house, for the family or housemates. The open door is a signal of hospitality and willingness to provide shelter. Granting of shelter has become a state institution. The oft demonstrated willingness to take people in has always been an indirect one. We wished with all our hearts that the state take in those who were true refugees. It was scandalous how this dilemma was instrumentalized by Lothar Späth and Franz Josef Strauss for their provincial campaigns in the late seventies and early eighties. As early as 1978 Lothar Späth inveighed against the "misuse" by the 33,000 asylum applicants of that year, approximately 7 percent of the 1992 statistic.

Ever since the Iron Curtain was raised the drama has radically transformed itself. The end of the dictatorships in Eastern

Europe has extended hope to countless people, as was the case 150 years ago, that rather than staying at home, they might be able to find a better life for themselves in the rich west. The crack in the door has been used toward this end. In unified Germany this is Article 16 of the Basic Law. Ironically enough, as dictatorships in the old style diminish in Europe and Asia, this article becomes increasingly attractive.

A cautious immigration policy for applications with an economic basis was more or less accepted during the sixties and seventies despite grumbling by the radical right. Five million people of non-German heritage became citizens. But now the twin terror of fear and hatred of foreigners has begun to grow as the repercussions felt at the agency charged with the social service of granting "shelter," i.e., the state, begin to effect the citizens themselves. In all the sad history of human migrations these have never occurred with democratic approval—in the cases involving a referendum, the indigenous population has always called for the gatekeeper. And despite this there have always been those quiet economic migrations: Poles to the Ruhr region, Huguenots to Prussia, Southern Europeans and Turks to the Federal Republic.

There is now the fear that those who come will disturb the peace with those who are already here, if not destroy it altogether: a responsibility of a new kind for citizens and politicians.

Appeals and demands for decency and openness are alone not enough. And yet we would not have a chance without this kind of public involvement, and it is crazy, if not cynical, to disparage and ridicule those who, despairing in the face of the hatred of foreigners, have taken up a banner against it.

The willingness to grant shelter is deeply rooted: over 70 percent of Germans are still in favor of political asylum. The high moral impetus (its execution, as we said, is delegated to the state) leads to special outrage when someone is caught sailing under the wrong flag. Mixed in with this anger is a bit of bad conscience, as well, that one is not really taking this willingness all that seriously or at least not seriously enough to make a personal sacrifice. The reason that the anger and then later the hatred for the "misuse" could be so easily fanned as early as a decade ago was a function of the fact that the task of "shelter" had been delegated to the state. Back then, though, the "misuse" was lost on people; it was easy to see through the laughable rightist propaganda: sixty million were supposedly incapable of taking in a few thousand refugees?

Now the immigrants are coming to a closed country with only one remaining emergency door: Article 16.

Lock and Key

At the present time many people are leaving the Social Democratic Party referring to the asylum debate as their basis, some speaking against, some for an amendment to Article 16. Many of the parting statements claim two different kinds of things—that the SPD leadership was supposedly maintaining a platform supported by perhaps 15 percent of the people, but should be able to wield the kind of power that would require the support of at least 95 percent of the citizenry in order to implement this platform. Mass immigration has never met with either a democratic solution or, for that matter, a democratic welcome. The mass immigration of German exiles was organized by military governments; following the unconditional capitulation, those countrymen of our own who had survived expulsion returned.

Five-million people live among us whom we consider "foreigners"—many are second-, some third-generation. The internal peace between them and people of German heritage has been entrusted to us. This peace with those who live among us must not be destroyed by the fear we have of the millions who will apparently yet come. This is our first obligation.

The democratic constitutional and administrative state is not only an instrument but consists of people. Whoever thinks that this state ought to come to terms with things by accelerated means and deportations of all sorts in the same manner, as might some highly efficient authoritarian structure, has failed to recognize that the democratic state can overtax itself: people just do not allow themselves to be marched off to Zirndorf in arbitrary numbers, police officers do not allow themselves to be permanently transformed into a deportation corp, people in the administrative courts do not allow their numbers to be arbitrarily increased. We citizens of the rich nations have all lost our innocence, hence our need to find the courage to face the following question: is it better for those seeking assistance and for democracy that we be a deporting nation or a rejecting nation? Our humanity is frayed in both cases. In a democracy there is no decree by the wise prince: "Be nice to one another." When the weave of democracy and the cultural life of tolerance have been torn apart no republic can mend it anew. Democracy is not the state of the wise, enlightened feudal lord who decrees that the Huguenots should be taken in. Democracy is a frayed yet stubborn weave, woven from common labor, from the balance between trust and mistrust, and often from the anger of the electing and the courage of the elected. Whoever tears at it maliciously can tear it apart, and he will not be able to restore it, at least not alone. And not within the course of a lifetime. In a cynical lack of responsibility, politicians on the right have until now considered this to be suitable grist for the election mill. The enticing drug of populism is addictive, but it is also life threatening. This is now being perceived by the CDU as well. In the FDP, district locals are moving closer and closer to the right-nationalist Jörg Haider, who wants to solve the for-eigner problem once and for all with a national referendum.

Things that on an ethical scale have been especially cherished, and for which people have fought, are that much more easily criticized if they can be used for criminal activity and organized crime. Every single asylum seeker who deals in drugs in Ham-burg damages the respect and tolerance to which thousands of other people of non-German heritage have rightful claim. Organized drug trafficking under the flag of right to asylum will kill this right in Germany. Hence we have to create a right to asylum which excludes its use for criminal purposes on this scale. The state was well prepared when it made the public claim that Poles had falsified their heritage in massive numbers in order to gain access to Germany via Article 16 of the Basic Law. It is difficult for us to come to terms with the fact these days that in Hamburg the right to asylum is being used on a massive scale for the drug trade. But that is the fact and it is difficult for us to admit this because the *Bildzeitung* can use it for its campaign as well.

I advocate amending the constitution for three reasons:

- I have worked for over thirty-five years to make Germany a home for people from distant lands. That is ten years longer than I have been a Social Democrat. I want to work on a reinstating of peace between those of German and non-Ger-man heritage.
- In the future as well people will need to come to us who are not suspected of a misuse of the law.
- In a democracy alliances between democrats must be possi-ble. Those who fundamentally reject dialogue with the other parties concerning a form of immigration policy can do noth-ing for those affected.

We can only counter violence by means of a large coalition of democrats. Of those who speak for an amendment to the Basic law, those who align themselves in support of the Rostock hooligans are in the minority. Those who want to protect minorites effectively require majorities.

But what is this business about identity? We did not clearly state to the people that the identities of their communities and city sectors would be radically changed by the storm of transformation. We are foisting upon people, those in the former GDR for instance, identity crises for which they were not prepared. We criticize the eccentric identity crisis of the new nationalist movements in Eastern Europe. We despair before the racist terror that is carried out by the Serbian army against everything non-Serbian. We easily distance ourselves when conservatives warn of the loss of identity in the singles culture that makes light of commitment but in reality yearns for it deeply. We are experiencing a hurricane of change in norms and values and suddenly the unique world experiment to give form to the idea of a global society, to give it a constitution and the power to enforce it has been transformed into a Social Democratic identity of yearning. I, too, mourn the fact that this does not function when faced with mass immigration, but I do not understand the aggression with which Article 16 has been declared a spiritual *life raft* in the storm of transformation. By making it precise democracy will not go under; without this precision it can.

Hearth and Home

Anxieties of foreign infiltration or control are not something to play down. I mean here the fear that one's own cultural forms of life might be transformed by all too many people from other cultures. They should not be played down if for no other reason than the fact that the explosive force of all-day, all-evening, and more recently all-night foreign television culture has eroded all forms of traditional home life, family stability, child-parent relations, regard for others, reliability vis-à-vis friends and respect for one's neighbors. No foreigner will ever touch the core of German family life as intimately as do television sex and television crime. Against these forces just try to preserve something of German cultural life and family traditions. Of course we should talk about fear of the other, the outsider, as well as the transformation of our city districts, but first we must call murder murder, and terror terror; we must call expulsion by its real name and condemn all of these practices. Then we can talk.

He who throws explosives through windows behind which people live condones the death of these people. He is a potential murderer. He who applauds potential murderers or even protects them from apprehension by the police is guilty of aiding and abetting.

He who gets excited about other people, about their children, about their ways of life, which are characterized by misery, may of course do so, but he who musters the understanding to realize that, on account of this anger, terrorist acts are being perpetrated does injury to all the constitutional standards of this democracy. And this regardless of the conditions under which the children, women, and men have sunk to the point that there is a desire to get rid of them again.

To react to the pogrom "with understanding" is almost as dangerous a brew as the explosives themselves which were tossed through the window:

There must not be understanding for such terror, not for a second, not by politicians, not by commentators. Rostock saw the terror of expulsion, and it met with ghastly success: the people targeted were removed. The whole world speaks of the "untenable" conditions and once again a large show of violent force and manifestation of terror is sanctioned by means of a "certain understanding."

Germany never did and never will correspond to that cozy family idyll that can only be found these days in living rooms whenever the perfectly dyed, white-haired granny wants to make a certain margarine or specific yogurt tasty for the happy little blond children (what old-fashioned German gobbledygook). The healthy German family can no longer be found outside of breakfast commercials. Politicians, publicists, and all those who need domestic tranquility as badly as they need air to breathe must finally make it clear to the populace: there are no longer any idylls to defend from foreigners. We have only ourselves to blame for our terrible High Speed Society that has sent values tumbling, that forces us to be forever reorienting ourselves, to be building the humanism of tomorrow out of the wreckage of yesterday and the ruins of today; for the terrifying pace of our (only technically) networked global society. Those people who are attempting to flee the hurricane of change in Southern Europe, in the Near East, or in Africa bear the least responsibility.

Translated by Martin Black

·6·

LETTER TO MY VIEWERS TO THE RIGHT OF THE SCREEN

ERNST ELITZ

Everyone likes to get nice letters, including those of us in television. But anyone who utters the words "asylum" or "foreigner" on the air nowadays risks a barrage of mail. And the letter writers, unfortunately, are not the friendliest of people. Many of them, in their outrage, forget to give their names and addresses. This reply is dedicated to them, but also to those whose behavior is postally correct.

Dear Viewer to the Right of the Screen,

Let me begin with a personal confession. I don't know any skinheads, nor anyone who openly professes to be a *Republikaner.** I don't know where one can buy an Imperial German war flag, nor records by "Werwolf" or "Stoerkraft." That is simply not my kind of music. But I don't think you would like it much yourself, since, as I assume from your handwriting, you are a member of the older generation. But that's just the way

---

*Member of an extreme right-wing party of the same name.

things are: the younger right makes noise, the older right writes letters. But I can't see too much difference in the text: "foreigners out" and "Germany for the Germans," I encounter it everywhere. A few of you have even had these sentiments made into rubber stamps, and decorate your letterheads with them.

In your letter you make the assumption that I have a nice house in the suburbs, and that there is no refugee camp bordering on my property. That is true. But within a thousand meters of my house there are two large shelters for asylum seekers, set up by the city authorities. Yet no one steals the laundry from the nice neighbors' clotheslines, no Sinti relieves himself in the garden of our housing complex. I only know that in the neighboring town, several young people under the influence of alcohol and of German nationality killed an Albanian. They thought he was a "Polack."

But now I'll talk about my work, in which you've expressed such interest. You complain that in my programs I only invite to speak those who are positively disposed toward foreigners. That is not my doing. When I invite Germans and foreigners to be in the audience of the "PRO & CONTRA" program, it is nearly always those who are positively disposed toward foreigners who choose to speak. The others would rather express their opinions in secret. They call me on the phone or write letters like you. "Too many filthy foreigners on the program" writes Mr. Huber from Konstanz. Those are surely your sentiments exactly. The same holds for Mr. Klink from Lauenburg, who shares your way of thinking and who can't understand how Germans could work for such a "radical, foreigner-loving station." "After all, you're being paid with our good German money," admonished one woman in a letter. One man commanded with military brusqueness: "Shut your trap!" he wrote, after I had spoken out in support of the basic right to political asylum. A colleague of mine who had likewise spoken out in support of this right received a postcard: "Stupid cow. Why wasn't Franz Schoenhuber* invited? He would have told you a thing or two."

You won't believe it, but Franz Schoenhuber himself showed up for our last election special. With the words "After all, we are colleagues," he shook my hand and offered a warm greeting. Then, this former executive of *Bayerischer Rundfunk* (Bavarian Broadcasting) took the major parties, who had finally adopted his policy against the "pseudo-asylum-seekers," to task. Was he totally off base? He wasn't.

The politicians from the major parties react just as irrationally to the foreigners as you do, and those like you, who have carried over a childish fear of the bogeyman into your adult years. The SPD in their infinite humanitarianism turned a blind eye to the waves of foreigners arriving from the poverty-stricken areas of the world. The CDU-CSU passed the problem on to an overworked bureaucracy, which soon gave up. The Minister of Defense refused to let the foreigners into the empty military barracks; they wouldn't have frightened the citizens so much there. And perhaps you, Dear Writer, would not have had the opportunity to vent your displeasure so vehemently.

Not even criminal asylum seekers were deported. If that had happened, your favorite newspapers would not have been able to continue stirring up fear of the "evil foreigners." The immigration offices were kept understaffed, so the lines of people waiting to get in got longer and longer. I remember seeing one such scene on television, of an immigration office just after they had opened in the morning; hundreds of asylum seekers tumbled head over heels into the offices. The image of the flood of asylum seekers could not have been staged better in a campaign spot for the *Republikaner*. Existing laws were not applied. Instead, the politicians called for an amendment to the Consti-

---

*Leader of the *Republikaner* party.

tution, to show at least rhetorically that they were capable of action. But every actor in this political farce will tell you confidentially that not even a constitutional amendment would change anything in practice. But in the *Bundestag* the speakers keep throwing smoke bombs. Once the smoke finally clears, the foreigners are still being hated, and the politicians lose even more credibility. That suits your Franz Schoenhuber just fine.

Fishing for applause, he can keep inveighing against the luxurious accommodation of foreign asylum seekers. The envious German claps and cheers. Dear Viewer to the Right of the Screen, do you really believe that the container colony surrounded by barbed wire is cozier than your living room with its knick-knacks and remote control, where you can choose between porno on one channel and burning refugee camps on the other, whichever suits your fancy? Which will it be today? Mr. Schoenhuber can keep invoking the specter of the fear of foreign criminals. With every purse snatching the good German points to the nearest asylum seeker. Whoever beats up blacks and slanty-eyed orientals is then a good guy. "The country is overflowing with people and garbage," writes Mr. Anonymous. And that's why the "youth of Rostock are not right-wing, they love their homeland and are for cleanliness." You'll certainly agree with that.

These fine young people are giving the Hitler salute again. And honestly, do you take offense at our showing these scenes every night? Naturally, viewers will call up and demand that we put a stop to these reports of attacks on refugee camps once and for all. They leave a bad impression abroad; and every stone-throwing incident, every Molotov cocktail only encourages imitation. Soon someone will maintain that there wouldn't be any antiforeigner sentiments at all if there weren't so much television coverage of the subject. But you also write that you aren't prejudiced against foreigners. It's just that the foreigners should stay where they are: Germany for the Germans, and the rest of the world for the filthy foreigners. Have I understood you correctly?

A few months ago, your young friends the skinheads demanded money for each man and each hand raised in the Hitler salute. I would have taken any colleague who paid even one penny for such a spectacle and tossed him out on his ear. But that's my personal opinion. Surely you have a different view of the matter. Anyone who yells himself hoarse for Germany needs money to lubricate his vocal cords afterwards. And skinheads don't drink Adam's ale, they drink German beer. I've done a bit of research into the matter. Nowadays, not even foreign television journalists give tips for the Hitler salute. You can get that for free nowadays, anywhere you want.

As for the letters that clutter my desk on the subject of foreigners, it's ten to one for people like you. We broadcast images of right-wing radical demonstrators shouting "Germany for the Germans! Foreigners out!" and you pay one mark in postage to applaud them. We commentators weigh out the pros and cons of a constitutional amendment. But you, the letter-writing viewer, are strictly in favor of deportation. Not some constitution, but the properly German-minded citizen should be the first and final authority in all matters concerning foreigners, you write. "We are the people!" scribbled one man in his letter. It didn't come from the East, that much I could infer from the postmark.

Recently, while reading my letters, I was able to sigh with relief. A Protestant woman wrote me. She is looking after a Kurdish family that is being threatened with deportation. "Don't let up on those rabble-rousers, please!" she wrote. "That gives me courage." You can't imagine how much pleasure that letter gave me. Now I'm even a little proud again to be a German.

Translated by Daniel Theisen

· 7 ·

IDLE THOUGHTS

PETER ESCHBERG

I am a foreigner, even if German is my native language. (I do not mean that in a whining sort of way, like those Germans who publicly demonstrate their undeserved solidarity with the "poor foreigners"—as though they wanted to assert that they themselves were better people.) I am a citizen of that nation that let itself be "brought back into the fold" in 1938. I have lived and worked for decades in Germany, which—not only artistically speaking—has become my second home. Recently I have been asking myself when it will be time to leave this country. I ask myself this for many reasons: because I can no longer stand the screams of the pillaging mobs I hear every day on television; because I no longer understand the politicians (or perhaps I understand them too well), who play their inscrutable games by inciting the rage of the masses; finally, because I no longer want to understand this self-forgetting people, the better part of which once belonged to the ranks of the asylum seekers themselves.

As a young man, I got to know emigrants, some eminent, some less so, in my native city of Vienna and later, in Munich. Their stories, for all the suffering they described in detail, always had for me something curiously distant and foreign about them—stories of terrible times that would never return. The documents of the emigration as well, the most moving of which is perhaps Kortner's film *Der Ruf,* spoke only for themselves, not to me. They would have spoken to me if I could have seen myself in the position of the heroes (or victims) of these stories, but this seemed impossible to imagine. And it was equally impossible for me to imagine what it can mean (or must mean) to leave one's country, one's friends, one's profession, one's language—and in the loneliness of a foreign country, a foreign language, a foreign culture, to begin a new life. This is the way I think today, looking back in skepticism. And this perhaps has to do with the fact that certain experiences that embrace the very limits of existence are by their innermost nature not communicable; all that can come across is a report, a story, an anecdote. Emigration—that seemed to me to be one of the extremes, one of the poles of antifascist resistance, the other pole being underground work in the enemy territory of one's home country. Flight and exile—those were political concepts, far removed (as it seems to me today) from all shabby day-to-day reality, precise ciphers of an existential decision against the inner enemy, exemplary sacrifices made in the name of humanity. The pathetic or comical practical wisdom contained in the films, books, and stories of the emigration was ennobled by the active antifascism of the creators of these works.

And thus, what I thought back then seems to me today quite lofty, abstract, and theoretical. Every idea stands or falls on the basis of banal details; I think of how it would be if it ever came time to leave Germany, and, remembering its history, to emigrate to a third country—and already the questions begin to present themselves. First—how does one know when the right moment has arrived? There are experiences one could learn from here, if only they were not the experiences of other people at other times. Some of those emigrants whose stories I have heard fled in time (i.e., quite early—or too early?), some quite late (almost too late or just in the nick of time). What determines the right moment to flee—the insight into the hopelessness of a political situation, the courage to take the necessary steps consistent with, and act according to this insight, or the fear of daring to put all one's energy into a seemingly impossible act of resistance? Another question: how does one organize one's flight into exile? What does a person leaving his circle need? Not one of us who has enjoyed fifty years of peace and prosperity is able to answer such simple, practical questions. What we do know, is not much: fleeing is not the same as traveling, for the traveler carries his home around with him; the fugitive has lost his old world and has not found a new one.

I admit, such questions are games of the mind—idle, frivolous, and yet sometimes urgent. Even when they become serious, when the situation becomes unbearably critical, they are miles away from their own resolution—perhaps they even hinder their own resolution. All the more dramatic, inconceivably dramatic, I imagine, must be the situation of people for whom such idle thoughts have become the starkest reality. And when the very notion of such a fugitive existence is almost unbearable for those like us, how is it then possible for people who live a secure existence not to understand the plight of other people who have given up everything to save their very lives, and to regard the helpless refugee as nothing but a rival, a parasite?

Perhaps humanity is not a moral category, but a function of the imagination—the ability to imagine the fate of another as one's own. So we have come full circle: I sometimes think a

political situation is possible that makes the peremptory demand of each individual that he entertain the notion that it is
high time to turn his back on this unimaginative country and
begin a new life somewhere else, where such a forced imagination is not necessary.

Translated by Daniel Theisen

·8·

GERMANS AND FOREIGNERS: PEACEFUL COEXISTENCE, NOT DISCRIMINATION AND VIOLENCE

HEINER GEISSLER

Burning refugee shelters, people being hunted like rabbits—these are the television images that in the past several months have been sent from Germany to all parts of the world, and they have had an impact. One out of every three jobs in Germany is directly tied to the export trade. That means that in large branches of trade, our wages depend on the purchase of our products by foreigners—people who live in other countries. If the impression starts to establish itself in the world that hatred of foreigners in Germany is again on the rise, then the end of our role as world champion in foreign trade could well be at hand, and it is upon this role that our prosperity depends. This is one of the lessons to be learned from the sad incidents in Rostock, Huenxe, and numerous other towns and cities: right-wing radical thugs, hooligans along for the ride, and cheering rubbernecks, are sawing off the branch they—and unfortunately the rest of us as well—are sitting on. Our prosperity depends to a large extent upon the image we project abroad. The president of the Association of German Chambers of Industry and Commerce has correctly observed that the German economy is being threatened with losses amounting to billions as a result of the outbreaks of right-wing violence.

At the beginning of September a Munich newspaper reported the following: "The deal was worth thirty million marks. That is the amount Song Yi, director of a Peking paper factory, had planned to spend in Germany for new machines. But the deal fell through. The Chinese businessman was accosted on the street in Berlin by a man who shouted at him and slapped him in the face. Mr. Song and his delegation left the country immediately, and ordered the machines in the USA." Unfortunately, as anyone who reads the newspaper knows, this is not an isolated incident. Every German businessman and politician who travels abroad and tries to encourage investment in Germany must submit to a barrage of questions about the political and social situation in our country and about our attitude towards foreigners, for the impressions left by foreign television coverage of the violence in Germany are deep ones. The Japanese ministry of foreign trade recommends that business travelers from that island country avoid certain urban districts in Germany and wear conspicuously elegant and European clothing in order to keep down the likelihood of being mistaken for Vietnamese asylum seekers or workers. One can easily imagine what conclusions the people concerned will draw from such advice. The flight to Frankfurt, booked on Lufthansa, is canceled, the hotel reservation is canceled, along with the working lunch in the restaurant. Personal contact with business partners, which, despite all the communication possibilities open to the business world is still as important as ever, is broken off; possibly the transaction as well.

Our economic interests are naturally not the main argument against brutality towards others. In a civilized nation of culture there is no justification at all for brutality towards people, for all people are endowed with the same dignity, no matter what their origin, their skin color, or their native tongue. The Constitution confirms this, for Article 1 does not state that "the dignity of Germans is inviolable"; explicit reference is made to "human dignity." Anyone who does not understand the moral arguments should at least be able to grasp the secondary arguments, the economic ones.

The growing political radicalism and its corollary, the growing willingness, especially by young people, to commit violent acts, is also the result of a nearly complete failure of our education system. One need not wonder that young people have lost nearly all moral constraints, when they hear nothing in the schools of God, of human dignity, or of the moral values of our society. Many young people do not even hear of these from their parents. The instilling of values must be made the first priority of our education policy. What we fail to invest in schools, education, and families today, we will pay tomorrow twice over for combating crime, but by then the baby will have already fallen into the well.

To look for scapegoats for one's own problems and to vent one's frustration on them is the stupidest thing one can do. Have we forgotten our own history? The Jews were the scapegoats for the Nazis. First the synagogues burned, then the whole world—including Dresden, Hamburg, Berlin, and Cologne. The "enemy of the working class" was the scapegoat for the Communists: first came the expropriations, then the wall, the barbed wire, and the order to shoot all escapees on sight. Should foreigners and asylum seekers have to be the new scapegoats?

Civil war refugees and the politically persecuted must continue to be afforded protection and refuge. The expansion of the basic right to political asylum does not stand in the way of this goal, but is necessary to achieve a European division of labor. But this will not get rid of the actual causes of the waves of refugees: namely poverty, civil war, environmental catastrophes, and the economic chaos that is following the collapse of the Communist empire. That is why we will have to take on refugees in the coming years as well, and the people have to be told this. Naturally, we cannot alleviate the plight of the world in the welfare offices of Dortmund, Stralsund, Hanover, or Erlangen. But neither is there any reason to sit back complacently in our armchairs and act as though the distress of the refugees in distant regions of the world were not our problem. What is needed is a comprehensive political plan by the Western countries to eliminate, as far as possible, the causes of the migration, and to take the corresponding steps to convince the public of this need. One cannot make the facts go away by ignoring them; only by having the courage to face the truth can lost trust be regained.

Additionally, the people in Germany will have to be told that in the future they will be living with more, not fewer foreigners. There is nothing wrong with that, either. Apart from the question of refugees and asylum seekers, economists and labor market experts—such as Norbert Walter, chief economist of the Deutsche Bank; Wolfram Engels, professor of economics at the University of Frankfurt; Max Wingen, former president of the statistical office of the state of Baden-Wuerttemberg; or Karl Proebsting, president of the state Labor Exchange of Nordrhein-Westfalen—predict that due to the decades-long slump in birth rates, we will in the foreseeable future be needing qualified immigrants to fill jobs and to pay into the pension coffers. They will help us overcome the difficult problems connected with the declining birthrate. It must be possible to live together with foreigners just as harmoniously as before Hoyerswerda, Huenxe, and Rostock, but hopefully even more so.

Whether the society of the future is called a "multicultural society" or not is not a primary problem, and as far as I am concerned, pseudoscientific behavioral experts and editorial writers can carry on heated debates about the matter. What matters are not concepts, but concrete plans. The society of the future must not be allowed to become a three-class society, with first, second, and third class people like in ancient Sparta. It must be a peaceful society of equality; after all, it is our children who will be living in it. It can only be built on the foundation of human dignity, mutual respect, tolerance, and the values of humanism and Christianity, as befits a civilized nation. Nobody can tell me that man, who can fly into space and split atoms and genes, should not be able to live peacefully with a Turk if he is German, or with a Moslem if he is a Christian, or with a black if he is white.

Translated by Daniel Theisen

·9·

SPECTER OF A
BROWN RESURRECTION

RALPH GIORDANO

We are experiencing a situation the likes of which we have not seen since 1945. Hostility toward foreigners is racing across Germany in epidemic proportions, a racist brushfire that, under an open sky and in the clear light of day, flaunts the tokens and emblems of National Socialism. In so doing it has already murdered over twenty people. And this is occurring to the applause of shameless onlookers as well as what are obviously considerable segments of the population alongside the feeble defensive of a state that has continued to boast of its power monopoly—a monopoly it did not hesitate to employ against the left, or what was thought to be the left, with the most excessive force. Today, by contrast, German right-wing radicalism is virtually able to deride and jeer the state and its organs with impunity, and this with full justification considering the meek, weak-kneed manner in which this paper tiger has dealt with the perpetrators in the past few months, the worst months yet. Yes, a specter is haunting united Germany, this third German Democratic Republic following Weimar and the former Federal Republic—the specter of a brown resurrection! This time, unlike its appearance in the mid-sixties, it is no temporary phenomenon, but is today deeply rooted in the society, and tomorrow will have established itself in the parliamentary structure at both the federal and provincial level.

Murder by flames in the history of Germany is not just some factory accident that will burn itself out on its own. There is a much more direct historical and political connection between the present activity of these mobile squads of German right-wing vandals and our failures of the past.

It is high time for drawing up a short balance sheet, one for the greater German Republic. But first let us review the former Federal Republic. Only now are the seeds of her second guilt bearing bloodied fruit, that of the repression and denial of Hitler after 1945. At the same site of the most infamous crime in recorded history, a crime of which it was well known that millions upon millions of victims were being slaughtered like insects *behind* the fronts of World War II, it was here that the biggest reintegration industry for the perpetrators was established. With only a few exceptions these perpetrators not only were let off in the end unpunished, but they were also allowed to continue their careers with impunity. The pre-1945 "experts of destruction" became, as a matter of course, the "experts" of the reconstruction, and well into the 1970s the elite of finance, industry, and government was almost identical to that under Hitler. Now for the first time the well organized amnesty white-wash of Nazi criminals is avenging itself on a catastrophic level, avenging itself for the virtually global absolution accorded them, to both large and small, from the desk job murderers of the holocaust to the bosses of the extermination apparatus as well as to the thousands of executioners in the Reich security headquarters under Keydrich and Kaltenbrunner. Though the instigator of the so-called Nuremberger race laws, Hans Globke was nonetheless the éminence grise of the Federal Republic's early years, the father of the federal chancellorship, intimate of Konrad Adenauer and under secretary of state. He has not been forgotten. Also unforgotten is Paragraph 131 with which almost the entire National Socialist bureaucratic structure was incorporated into the democratic administrations; unforgotten is the number of Hitler's diplomats, his one-time economic minister for defense and his director of the military who were allowed to proceed with their careers from promotion to promotion; unforgotten above all is that not one of the NS killing judges or attorneys ever has been convicted by a federal court, an indelible blemish on the Second German Democracy.

And right next door, born, in a manner of speaking, of the same class, was the former GDR with its superficial "mandate on antifascism," a one-party, misbegotten state nurtured by the adventurous lie that it was somewhat of a covictor of World War II, in fact a part of the anti-Hitler coalition. It is a simple matter of logic that the GDR's national leadership, on both theoretical and material grounds, shirked its German responsibility for Nazism and the holocaust, fell completely into step with the party line of Soviet-Stalinist anti-Semitism and practiced a pronouncedly anti-Israeli foreign policy. We are experiencing now the glowing embers of all these life lies, the results of those erasures that the internal ruling class of the socialist East left behind in the historical consciousness of its people. Today the noxious brew that has been festering under the deceptive lid of "mandated antifascism" is beginning to explode, and the murderous consequences are obvious. Germany, your criminals! There must be no hearing granted *those* voices that maintain that what is presently scandalizing the entire world is

mere happenstance, could take place anyplace, is a concentration of miserable circumstances, independent and detached
from the aggregate condition of the rest of society. No, and
again no! The tornado of racist hostilities toward outsiders and
foreigners, this entire renaissance of an unbridled proclivity for
violence capable of every form of murderous mayhem, all of
this is deeply rooted in that *second* guilt of repression and denial
with which both German "half-states" each encumbered themselves under their respective banners.

At the same time it would be foolish for us to proceed as if
the foreigner and immigrant issues were not really problems or
were easily solved—this they would not be even with goodwill,
the best of wills. It would also be wrong to make light of the
fears and anxieties of German nationals, to ignore them fully,
denounce them as hostile and hold all views opposite to one's
own as already criminal. Take care! But as legitimate as various
opinions are on how the larger problem of immigration is to
be solved there must be basic consensus on the following four
points:

1. Germany has de facto long been a country of immigrants
   and must now finally officially acknowledge this.
2. The acceptance of political refugees must remain unal-
   tered in the basic law as a humanitarian charter.
3. All arrivals must be treated with human dignity, and
4. This, too, in capital letters: for racism, hostility toward
   foreigners and resulting acts of violence there is not the
   slightest justification, neither a social nor a political one,
   neither a historical nor a moral one.

We are acquainted with the customary rationale on which
the perpetrators of violence and their sympathizers base their
arguments: unemployment, social frustration, an actual or pu-

tative lack of perspective. The degree to which they correspond to reality is difficult to admit; these claims cannot simply be swept under the carpet. These living conditions demand nothing less than immediate attention, and are the lot of far too many. But whoever draws the conclusion that these conditions are a justification for building firebombs and tossing Molotov cocktails at the inhabitants of shelters for foreigners and asylum seekers must have it made clear to them in no uncertain terms that they are not revolutionaries, not martyrs, not national heros; they are nothing but potential murderers!—And this must be made clear to them using the full force of the law and the visible common will of society. But—let us not deceive ourselves: the pretexts for practicing violence are interchangeable! Today it is this, tomorrow that. Does anyone believe that German right-wing radicalism would dissolve into thin air were the foreigner and immigration problem to find a solution? A new target would simply be selected—the fantasies of racist violence are unlimited and every one of their asserted motivations a fraud.

All too many announcements from the ranks of government representatives and politicians are a fraud—it is frightening. It is frightening when the assertions that the present danger is coming from the right are straightforwardly denied. Such was the case, for example, when the minister president of Mecklenberg-Vorpommern maintained that the arsonists of Rostock were not rightists at all, but rather identical with the protestors from Mutlangen, Brokdorf, and the Frankfurt airport's *Startbahn West*. . . .

If it had really been like that, if leftists had really torched and murdered, then the whole uproar would have long been over, then this state would have struck back in quite a different fashion, a second Stammheim story already neatly wrapped and tied.

One can only ask oneself: what kind of dark intention lurks behind this conscious distortion, behind this reversal of the facts? And what kind of perspective permits such disingenuousness in an attempt to have done with the racial brushfire? For decades the officials of the former Federal Republic raged against the "rule of the street," whenever it concerned leftists, or those considered to be such. But today, since in broad tracts of Germany rule of the "street" has actually become a reality, only this time by the right, there the powerful sit, indecisive, perplexed, full of sympathizing understanding for the poor, socially neglected and, at base, regrettable "victims" of this deplorable state of affairs—it is the kind of language as might be directed toward wayward relatives.

To the true victims in the homes and houses under attack, to those burned, those beaten, those beaten to death, there exists by contrast not the slightest hint of a more intimate relationship.

What is actually going on in this Germany? Who is still surprised by the perverse idea of celebrating in Peenemünde with champagne and caviar the fifty-year anniversary of the first successful firing of V-2 rockets that cost thousands of concentration camp prisoners and Londoners their lives? And who would try to convince us that the same criminals who used a remote-control device to blow up the Jewish museum on the site of the former concentration camp Sachsenhausen-Oranienburg outside of Berlin would not be inclined to kill Jewish people as well?

To state the case openly with its full ramifications: In the course of a rampant racism with interchangeable targets of aggression as well as interchangeable pretexts, a new situation is taking shape, not only for foreigners, but for holocaust survivors as well and for their families. It is characterized by an apparently inborn systemic weakness vis-à-vis rightist extremism. This has been confirmed recently in virtually terrifying manner. I am reminded of the parade in Thuringia's Rudolstadt on the occasion of the fifth anniversary of Rudolph Hess's death, Hitler's one-time deputy, as well as similar demonstrations in the Upper Franconian city of Bayreuth and in Wunsiedel in Lower Saxony. Although none of the three demonstrations had been issued permits, they nonetheless were granted permission to take place by none other than the highest German authority of justice, the Federal Constitutional Court. The Weimar Republic sends its greetings! One ought to contemporize what happened there and imagine what would have befallen anti-Nazi demonstrations in Weimar had they collided with the highest juristic decisions.

Uneasiness on our part, even in the most extreme, would no longer be a proper reaction, the less so since the room in which to operate granted the right-extremist mob can no longer be explained merely on the basis of poor organization or a reaction deficit. Obnoxious belittlement of the contemporary variant of National Socialism by high politicians, the lip service of feigned abhorrence and a relativizing sympathy for the culprits—these command the field.

By means of television everyone in these weeks has become a witness to it: the state has been notoriously defamed by the violent right; made ridiculous, totally jeered—but the head of intelligence was not ashamed to trivialize the whole thing, to minimize it and maintain that the problem was "well in hand." According to this version, the perpetrators themselves are merely the outer fringe of the media spectacle. To them is attached a second ring, a ring equally visible that enjoys public agreement with additional segments of the population. The third ring, comprised of the political organizers of German right-wing extremism, is no longer very visible, and the fourth ring not at all, an inner ring that spins out its connective web to high-level sympathizers and, by all accounts, can consider itself secure in their protection.

It is not incautious to say, with the racist hostilities toward foreigners and their bloody repercussions, that a new age threatens to dawn for the survivors of the holocaust as well for the entire Jewish community in unified Germany, for anti-Semitism is, of course, always involved. The appeal to our instinct to flee, which the Nazis instilled in us, has dramatically increased! Nothing has startled me in recent times so much as did the concerned question put to me by a Jewish friend: "Will I have to emigrate again," he asked; "will Germany once again force me to flee? Must I again fear for life and limb?" These words were spoken before a background of his initial emigration in 1935 and a return in the midsixties. This is what it has come to. I wish to bring to the attention of the German public that among the inhabitants of Jewish elderly and old-age homes the fear spreads that they could become the next target for aggression by the perpetrators of violence. This is new, a physical dimension of Jewish fear in Germany.

Since its christening in 1949 the former Federal Republic was anyway never really able to protect the survivors of the holocaust on a psychic level. For decades the Jews, whose members were murdered in the gas, had to read at the neighborhood newsstand that they were indulging in a hallucination if they had been mourning the loss of their kinsmen, because Auschwitz was nothing but a lie reproduced in print millions of times over the past thirty-five years in the name of democratic freedom of press and speech. And then finally when, much too late, the liars propagating the "Auschwitz lie" were prohibited by law from publishing their thesis, it then became apparent that this helpless prohibition comprised only half of the punitive ruling. The other half consisted of the threat of the same consequences for anyone caught publicly denying the expulsion of

Germans after 1945. Have you ever heard a word about an "expulsion lie"? Is it possible to imagine something more infamous, to think up such a depraved method as this in order to relativize Auschwitz? And this does not even take into account that the propagators of the "Auschwitz lie" have, in the meantime, found a hundred ways nonetheless to disseminate their atrocities "with full legal impunity" as it is called in Gerhard Frey's circle. I repeat, that with the extensive renunciation to counter right-wing radicalism by the otherwise avowedly eager exercisers of the state power monopoly, a new and dangerous chapter has been opened for the Jews in Germany. Were this republic to reserve only a fragment of the notorious militancy it has directed at leftist culprits and train it upon the right as well, then these new fears would not have arisen.

Now, however, they are here, along with those of foreigners in this country, and this brings up questions that ought to be placed publicly: is the Germany of today willing and in a position to put a speedy end to the brown specter? Or is it no longer able to banish these ghosts that have escaped out of the genie's bottle of the second guilt and mandated antifascism? Will Germany become dangerous again? Will it, for a third time, go down its own "special path"? Do people actually realize how thin the carpet will prove to be beneath which lie the common memories of those peoples at one time under German occupation, should the Schönhubers and Freys be elected into the next, the thirteenth Federal Parliament? Do they realize that it is simply not the same to talk about Le Pen's entrance into the parliamentary structure of France as it is to speak of the permanent integration of old and new Nazis into the Federal Parliament of united Germany? Most importantly of all: will it be repeatedly confirmed that in times of crises and emergencies Germany slides far to the right, irrespective of all historical experience, and that nothing can come of this but blood and tears? Will the mistrust confirm that, in the end, Germany will yet prove to be a fair-weather democracy and that, when the economic and social indicators forecast storms, large masses of voters really will seek shelter once again under the roof of the brown abomination of former times? And finally: would not the limit of the tolerable already be far exceeded were a grand coalition to prove to be the only means in the approaching elections to prevent organized right-wing radicalism from tipping the scale of the parliamentary balance?

So much for the questions.

Now for statements: should the Jews in Germany lose faith in this state, should they come to the definitive conclusion that the Third German democracy is not in a position to provide for the personal security of all peoples living within its borders—be they Jews or non-Jews, members of both sexes, peoples of all ages, nationalities and heritages—if, then, this loss of trust were to catch hold among Germany's Jews, then we would have much more on our hands than the emergency reaction of a community of between only 30,000 to 35,000 members among 75 million. A seismograph of this type would much more tend to indicate the oscillations of a political tremor by which the entire German society could once again be shaken.

I warn those responsible in the apparatus of this state not to underestimate the determination of the survivors of the holocaust, faced with new dangers to life and limb, to protect themselves and their families. Never again will we stand defenseless before our deadly enemies—never again! I warn the trivializers among the police, in the intelligence community, in the provincial parliaments, in the Federal Parliament and in the government to take stock of the degree of our resolve.

I confess that the events of the past year have altered my personal relationship to Germany. Until then I was of the opinion that concerning the matter of the second guilt, that of the repression and denial of the first under Hitler, the grand peace made with the perpetrators and their virtual amnesty despite all the intolerability, was, in the end, a matter of forced retreat by a power whose world-historical zenith had been reached in the first half of this century. Out of this arose as well, in like manner, the oft-promulgated confidence that, after all that had transpired, a Nazi triumph in a modern German incarnation was no longer possible. In the united Germany of 1991 and 1992 I have completely lost this confidence. It has made way for an open future about which I fear that the German state and its organs will conduct itself with increasing opportunism in respect to right-wing radicalism the more influential its voting potential becomes. For me a presumed certainty has hereby been revealed as an illusion, at least for the time being.

Nonetheless this should not be misunderstood as a lamentation, as an expression of resignation or as an urging to surrender. On the contrary—the opposing force must be doubled, my own as well. I can draw no other lesson. And hence I profit from the fact that the purgatorial flames of Nazi racial hatred have made me wholly incapable of capitulation.

In concluding I would like to make myself understood on one other matter: not one of my sentences, not one of my words, not even with one letter of a word have I intended to speak here of *the* Germans! Rather I am counting on a broad array of like-minded citizens in the fight against racist xenophobia and right-wing radicalism. I am counting on those who know that they too are threatened when *we* are threatened. Let no one believe that racial hatred and anti-Semitism is directed only against Jews—these things are directed toward all those who are not nor wish to be as the anti-Semite would have them be.

Let us close ranks with the foreigners under attack and unite with humane Germans. Their numbers are many. Let us seek out allies beyond our borders and lend strength with this inter-national to what is obviously the most benign of government evils in the history of humanity—the democratic republic and its precious, ever-endangered freedoms.

Translated by Martin Black

·10·

LOOKING FOR THE RIGHT TONE

ALFRED GROSSER

It is difficult to find the right tone. It is not a matter of repeating what is said in France every time a crisis involving Germany arises: "Should we be afraid of the Germans? Certainly not! But should we be afraid *for* the Germans? There *are* reasons for that. But this fear can only be fruitful if we feel it in empathy with the Germans, in solidarity." Neither is it a matter of taking an indignant stand against the outside observers always ready to pounce on what they perceive as the negative in Germany, who then triumphantly or with honest concern announce: "So they *are* incorrigible, just as we have been saying all along!" I am reminded of a rabid article by the American journalist A. M. Rosenthal in the newspaper *Die Zeit* (October 2, 1992): "The Western politicians lied. Germany *is* dangerous." Or Elie Wiesel.

The constant complainers and accusers have been encouraged and confirmed in their complaints and accusations for decades by all those who in the Federal Republic of Germany emphasize only the negative and who portray themselves as the only Germans aware of the past, the only ones with a conscience—from the "new German cinema" to Günter Grass.

I am also certain that the tone of the much more numerous Germans is wrong who indulge in the two national sports—conceit (but the French are the champions in that!) and self-pity (in which Germany most likely deserves the gold medal)—is the wrong one. First example: the lamenting of the German mark's impending loss of brilliance, should it be subsumed under a European currency. Who mentions the benefits that would have resulted if such a currency had existed in October 1990? The other eleven European Community members would have prevented the German government from financing the reunification solely through going into debt, and the Bundesbank would not have to hinder all economic upswing in Europe, as they are doing today, by setting high interest rates.

Second example, which has to do with a more essential issue: the inability, not to mourn, but to compare. The West Germans want to keep on living as though there were no national duty to help their new fellow citizens become more equal. To do this, one would have to look constantly to the eastern regions of Germany. This is exactly what the Union of Civil Servants and Transportation Workers and the Metal Workers' Union are not doing. And in East Germany, it is to the West, not to the East, that people look for comparison, so the bitterness that exists in Warsaw or Prague is not perceived. Not only for the reason that of all the countries once dominated by the Soviet Union, only a single one can be assured of attaining affluence, and that this country is after all the heir to a previous Germany, without which there would not have been any Soviet soldiers in Poland or Czechoslovakia in the first place. Also because the unemployed in East Germany receive benefits that the unemployed in Poland would not even dare to dream of.

To say all this is simple. It is more difficult to let outrage and soberness prevail simultaneously. Outrage at hate and violence, mixed with deep concern, after I read a report in the supplement to the weekly magazine *Das Parlament* (September 11, 1992). The "extreme right-wing orientation of the East German youth" goes much further than one would be led to believe by a few skinheads. Not that the majority would make outrageous statements and pass them off as their own opinions, but the minority is growing; much more so among trade apprentices than among university preparatory school students. Are the outbreaks of hate and violence by young and old worse than in Great Britain or France? The answer is yes—but more so in the "new territories" (i.e., former East Germany). The legacy of a regime that instills hate in its subjects is therefore a double one. That the object of hate may have changed does not entitle one to speak only of the Nazi tradition and not of Margot Honecker.

But the outrage should not only be provoked by the excesses. My outrage, at any rate, is also provoked by the way Articles 116 and 16 of the Constitution are being interpreted in Germany, particularly in Bonn and Munich. How can one fight racism when one's own thoughts and actions are *"völkisch"*? (adjective, taken from Nazi terminology, denoting dedication to the ideals and interests of one's own—in this case the "Aryan"—race) Article 116 was placed towards the end of the Constitution because it was meant to solve a transitional problem: the Germans who were deported from their Eastern European homelands after World War II were to be given immediate citizenship in the new Federal Republic of Germany. A young Turk born in Frankfurt, however, who has never been to Turkey and who speaks not a word of Turkish has but a very slim chance of ever becoming a German citizen.

When I am asked in Germany, "What do you do in France about the young foreigners?" I answer, "I don't understand the question. We don't have any young foreigners. We *do* have hundreds of thousands of young, Islamic French citizens." Now should I tell my German audience in a calm tone or an exasperated tone how astounding it is that they completely failed to take notice of the figures that were published in the federal government's *Bulletin* of October 7, 1992? In the first nine months of the year there were 320,000 petitions for political asylum. The federal government made decisions on 155,000 of the cases. The acceptance rate was 4.6 percent! During the same period, 295,000 people from the Soviet Union, Poland, and Romania submitted applications to be allowed to immigrate on the basis of German ethnicity.

Article 16 is by no means exclusively devoted to foreigners. Only the words "Politically persecuted individuals have the right to asylum" apply to foreigners. There is no reason why the hows, whys, and wherefores should not be determined by a law. And yet what an enormous hypocrisy has been characterizing the German discussion of a "necessary" constitutional amendment! When the very discussion itself strengthens the convictions of those who object to the amendment! It is nevertheless better to outline this dispassionately, so that my words do not completely fall on deaf ears. . . .

I must confess here that it is neither the outbreaks of hate nor the application of Articles 116 and 16 that concern me most. Two other phenomena impress me more. Neither of the two is "typically German," but both have a particularly dramatic effect in Germany today.

The first one has to do with the constant underestimation, the constant brushing aside by the media, who only cherish the negative, and by the political and intellectual "elite," of that which is positive and encouraging. Hundreds of school classes vie for the President's Prize in the essay contest sponsored by the Koerber Foundation. The topics are hope inspiring: the history of one's native city during the time of Hitler, the positive things that foreigners have done or brought about, and now, for 1993, "Monuments: Remembrance, Warning, Nuisance." The regional parliament of Baden-Wuerttemberg sponsored an essay contest for students of high school age and below on the topic of "Living Together with our Foreign Fellow Citizens." Many students participated, German as well as foreign, and many moving essays were submitted. But who knows of this? Where is it being reported?

In Germany, more so than in France, thousands of men and women are sacrificing their time and energy for very little money working for organizations that help young people and the disadvantaged. But who knows of this? Where is it being reported?

For little money: this brings us to the second phenomenon. Just how can someone complain about the aggressive youth and their loss of values when he himself does not respect the basic values being referred to in his complaint? Freedom, justice, solidarity: how beautiful the common basis of the Christians and the godless humanists! Only the freedom for which the Chinese students died, for which many young and not-so-young people in the East in 1989–90 risked their lives, is really not our freedom. To risk one's own freedom for the freedom of others, for justice for others, for solidarity with others—this is the exact opposite of the freedom to which we are exhorted by advertisements hundreds of times every day: "Freedom consists in letting yourself go. Look out for number one. Do whatever you want—even if it's the opposite of what you wanted yesterday." The others? They simply do not exist. The important thing is the money everyone has, which enables one to buy the maximum amount of pleasure.

What does that have to do with the topic at hand? Plenty! The very act of speaking out against hate, of expressing outrage at those who "let themselves go" through violence should presuppose living the values in whose name one judges and condemns the haters, the perpetrators of violence. This applies particularly to the former East Germany, where the intellectual and emotional collapse has of course been more complete. And the Federal Republic of Germany could set such a good example here. The participants at the convention of the National Association of German Newspaper Publishers in Berlin most likely broke out in sympathetic or ironic smiles when they heard Foreign Minister Klaus Kinkel say in a speech—in my opinion an excellent speech: "The moral-ethical basis of our foreign policy is to be found in our Constitution." And yet, he was right. The Federal Republic of Germany had the good fortune not to have come into being as a nation, but, in the name of the rejection of two totalitarian systems—one in the past, and one in the neighborhood—to have been founded upon an ethic. The unified Germany could and should remain true to this ethic: to set an example for its partners, and as a remedy for the events and the attitudes that have been causing us so much concern.

Translated by Daniel Theisen

·11·

A SUGGESTION IN THE SPIRIT OF JACOB GRIMM

PETER HAERTLING

In 1848, as the German Parliament convened to create for themselves a progressive constitution, one Member of Parliament held it as absolutely necessary to place an article of his own creation before Article 1, which addresses the issue of human dignity. He wrote the following motion:

As Article 1, to be inserted before Article 1 of the draft, which would then become Article 2: "The German people is a people of free men, and German soil tolerates no servitude. Unfree men from abroad who dwell thereon, shall be made free." This provides a luminous frame for the human dignity being referred to. And German soil is not that "homeland" in its naive, ideologically narrow-minded sense, but a refuge for those who want to be free. What an offer! How naturally is

Germany being referred to here, how openly, and without a trace of swaggering, without a trace of arrogance. That is how the truly free speak. Jacob Grimm's motion was defeated in the National Assembly with a majority of thirteen votes.

In 1945 I was thirteen years old. The war, World War II, had taken away my parents. My father, a lawyer, had resisted Hitler quietly and courageously. My mother was not of pure "Aryan" blood. And I, as a little Nazi, as a member of the Hitler Youth, wrongly took it upon myself to stand up to my parents. When the war was over, I was still wearing the uniform; in the name of Hitler and of my people, millions of Jewish citizens had been killed, as well as Sinti, Romanies, political opponents, and homosexuals; it was at this time that the adults showed me just how quickly and without consequence one can forget. Those who had previously spouted Nazi ideology became model democrats, penitent Christians—at any rate successful people in the land of the blossoming economic miracle.

I have been leery of these quick-change artists to this day. But a few people told our story to others, and as the Constitution of the Federal Republic of Germany, the "Basic Law," was being written, they remembered—the experience was still burning in their memories—all those who had been persecuted, all those who had sought asylum, had gone into exile, and they formulated for Article 16, Paragraph 2, a great, magnanimous sentence: "Politically persecuted individuals have the right to asylum."

A door opens. The history of a people, for reasons of conscience, lays claim to its rights.

This article was *not* rejected.

Now, after forty-three years of constitutional reality, it faces being talked to pieces and repealed—according to the wishes of democrats who are the sons and daughters of the persecutors, and sometimes of the persecuted as well.

I hope that all those who think historically and all those who tell stories speak out against this unhistorical intention, which is a humiliation and a disgrace to us all.

No to you repressors, to you forgetful ones!

No to you selfish ones, polished clean by your success!

No!

And no to the young people, who in our country are yet again persecuting people, humiliating the weak, and setting fires.

But this *no* must encompass history; again, our history. When these young people speak and act in the name of Hitler, they are doing so in opposition to our repression, to our industriousness, to the lies they have had to endure, to assert their identity. The terrible children of Rostock and Wismar were led to believe that antifascism in East German society was a patent remedy, like capitalism in the West—a patent remedy for loss of memory. After a regimented upbringing, the children fell into a freedom that nobody explained to them, a freedom that quite possibly—and this should be a warning to us—nobody wanted to or could explain to them. Thus did they—those who had become weak—seek out their enemies from among the weaker, and find their slogans where their fathers and grandfathers had remained silent.

I call upon all of us, in the name of Jacob Grimm! Upon all of us free men and women on free ground. Not that we could or would want to give everything away, but we have a lot to give! And a portion of our dignity to defend. I call upon us every one, to afford refuge to those who are being persecuted by torturers, by ideologues, by murderers, by hunger. "Politically persecuted individuals have the right to asylum."

Should this article ever be repealed or replaced by empty rhetoric, then Germany, which with great difficulty but certainly not unhappily has come together again, will lose the foundation of a history that could in fact unify us.

We are submitting to those who are either fat and complacent or who are bloodthirstily awaiting their chance to eliminate us from the Right.

No! "German soil tolerates no servitude. Unfree men from abroad, who dwell thereon, shall be made free."

Translated by Daniel Theisen

· 12 ·

RACISM IS NO VENIAL SIN

PETER VON OERTZEN

All of us knew that in our people—as, by the way, is the case for the peoples in all of our neighboring countries—an active undercurrent of resentment, prejudice, and animosity towards foreigners exists. We remember the malicious epithets about "Ithaker" (derogatory expression for Greeks and Italians), "garlic eaters," or derogatory expressions for blacks. Over the past decades we have become familiar with the complaints of the foreigners living among us about ordinary, day-to-day discrimination. We found it nasty, mean, and disgusting; but honestly, nobody believed in any real danger to the foreigners among us, any real danger to the inner peace of our country—as cold and unfriendly as this peace may have been. And now, for the past year—more or less, it does not really matter—we have seen rowdy mobs chasing after "the others" almost every day with rocks, clubs, and Molotov cocktails. We have seen upstanding citizens applauding the spectacle, or at least standing on the sidelines and showing tacit approval by their silence. We have seen that the much-touted "true democracy" of the Constitution seems unable to defend itself, unable to stop this appalling spectacle. We have seen that the political leaders of this country—the members of the so-called political class—are incapable of sweeping the mob from the streets and effectively protecting our foreign guests. We have seen that they cannot even manage to place the moral pestilence of xenophobia under quarantine, but instead are shrinking back from it step by step. The pitiful squabbling over the right to political asylum is a sign of this; much worse, however, is the attitude expressed by the following sentiment: "Of course, we are against violence in any form (who knows where that would lead?), but then again, we can see where these people are coming from. After all, the boat is full!"

I admit in all honesty that two years ago, I did not believe that something like this could be possible in our "civilized" country—not even one year ago, after it had long since started. What happened? We must answer this question before we can find an answer to the other question: What do we have to do?

All references to unsolved economic and social problems, to unemployment, to the lack of housing, neglected housing projects, to the lack of perspective among young people, to dull despair over the lost sense of security in the former East Germany: all of these offer useful insights. They can account for protests, voter apathy, demonstrations, strikes, even riots. It is also quite obvious that scapegoats are being sought. But still, the question remains: Why foreigners? And of all foreigners, why these foreigners? Why asylum seekers in particular? In recent years, Germany has taken on more than a million ethnic Germans from Eastern Europe. Then, too, there were protests, unfriendliness, spitefulness; but there was nothing that could compare with the present excesses against the asylum seekers. Yet the ethnic German emigrants, who of course are full-fledged German citizens, were (and still are) to a much greater extent than the asylum seekers real competitors for jobs, apartments, and state benefits. So why?

Let us turn the question around. Suppose as a result of some catastrophic political, economic, or social development, seven hundred thousand Swedish, Danish, English, or Irish people flooded the shelters or the offices of the public relief agency in Zirndorf, and laid claim to apartments, counseling, and relief payments from the public coffers. Suppose that only 10 percent of them or less had really been politically persecuted; the rest of them being "pseudo-asylum seekers," driven to emigrate by economic necessity. Would they also have to endure rocks, clubs, and Molotov cocktails every night, would we hear that same half-hearted "Well, we basically understand the people, but. . . ."? To ask the question is to answer it. White skin, light hair, blue eyes, Christian, customs similar to ours, same eating habits—no problem, at least no serious problem. But these refugees: brown, yellow, or black, Moslem or God knows what, different foods, different customs, possibly even "Gypsies"? No, "the boat is full!"

There is no way around the bitter truth: what is boiling up out of the depths of the souls of a part of the German population—the smaller part, I still hope—is nothing other than racism. It is that fundamental feeling that tells people: "Of course all people are equal, only some are more equal than others; namely US and those like US."

Hitler notwithstanding, racism is not a specifically German phenomenon. It exists in the U.S.A. and in Great Britain, in France and in Italy, in Asia and elsewhere as well (the treatment of the "Untouchables" in India and the Eta in Japan shows racist tendencies). But this in no way exonerates us; our racism is our problem—particularly since Hitler.

Rejecting and derogating others, attributing their "otherness" to biological "fact," all the way to denying their very humanity—i.e., racism—has always been a source of conflicts, discrimination, oppression, and cruelty. Most of the great philosophers, sages, and founders of religions have for this reason denounced racism: before God and the moral law, all people are equal (though the churches brought into existence by those great founders were not always quite so free from racial prejudice). But in our day and age, racism is more than just morally reprehensible; it is suicidal. Economically, politically, socially, and culturally, humanity is growing together irreversibly into a unified world society. One does not need to rave and gush naively about the "multicultural society" to see that humanity itself is in fact multicultural, and that we will never be able to survive together if we do not learn to accept "the others" as our equals and to live with them in decency.

The idea of an ethnically homogeneous state, in which one people, one "race," one religion, one culture exists completely unto itself, has by now become an illusion and is becoming ever more so. Germany is not to become a land of immigration? What self-deception! Germany already *is* a land of immigration! Or does anyone really believe that the "guest workers" and their families—more than five million people—will ever disappear? On the contrary: in the course of European unification, in the course of the inevitable opening up to Eastern Europe, the number of "aliens" in our midst will continue to increase. And we are going to have to learn to live with them and their "otherness," or else face the consequence of self-destruction.

Racism, however, destroys the moral and social foundations of such a coexistence. And that is why the problem of racism is not, as some assert, a question of "right" or "left." Whatever these concepts may still mean, racist tendencies exist even among the traditional supporters of the "left," and upright resistance to racism among those of the "right." Or are the major Christian churches, which have been actively opposing the undermining of the right to political asylum, all of a sudden "leftist?"

What is needed is a reestablishment of the post-Hitler consensus that racism is not a venial sin, but a disgrace—and that shrinking back from it is suicidal. And from the powers of state we must demand that they put a decisive stop to the pogroms— the youthful mob, by the way, understands the language of the strong arm quite well. As nuclear energy opponents and pacifists took to the streets, the "able-bodied democracy" struck back with a vengeance. We certainly do not want to see a repeat performance of such an abuse of power. The simple application of existing laws will suffice—but quickly, decisively, and with all due severity.

Translated by Daniel Theisen

·13·

VOICES AGAINST THE RIGHT

FRITZ PLEITGEN

It is with great dismay that we Germans have been observing the spectacle of the Balkan sister nations' killing each other off. Our shock is great, and it is honest. Yet at the same time, we are overlooking the bloodthirstiness that is growing like a cancer in our own country.

Foreigners, who are fleeing unbearable conditions in their homelands, are being threatened in Germany with insults and firebombs. A disgrace for our people, no doubt, but one could argue that it does not compare to the atrocities being committed in the former Yugoslavia. Yet we need only imagine how quickly we Germans would escalate our malicious behavior if the asylum seekers were actually to put up a serious fight for their right to stay.

Not a pretty thought. But why the casual reference to "we Germans?" Collective guilt—that has of course long since been rationalized out of our past. We should not have any trouble making short shrift of all collective responsibility for the future either. Besides, is it admissible to lump together all Germans with an—admittedly—growing number of primitive brutes? After all, there are more than a few upright democrats who have been raising their voices against xenophobia and right-wing radicalism. But what are these voices really accomplishing? Quite possibly, next to nothing.

What could help would be thousands of instances of civil courage and commitment—setting a personal example by taking in foreigners in distress. Whoever finds this too much should at least contribute time and energy to some cooperative venture to provide shelter and support to those in need. Backed up by such exemplary acts, the battle for the souls of open and clandestine sympathizers of the brutal right-wing extremists could be taken up with good prospects for victory.

The same strategy could be used to defend Article 16, an exemplary article in our Constitution. But since here and there (or perhaps more than we think) the energy and the strength of character do not suffice for such action, our own weakness forces us to search for the guilty parties. They are quickly found. They are, as always, the politicians, who of course through their actions set themselves up as such unmistakably.

They did not overlook the asylum problem, let alone suppress it. On the contrary, they quickly made it into a public matter, so as to make their differently minded political opponents look bad—to make them appear as either antidemocrats or as undutiful guardians of the civic peace.

The embarrassing and never-ending party squabbling led the German constitutional state into the morass from which right-wing radicalism now draws its criminal energies. Ever since, reports of burning refugee shelters and of acts of violence against foreigners and Jews have become everyday news items in the new Federal Republic of Germany.

We have no lack of empathy, but it is more empathy with ourselves than with those being persecuted on German territory. What worries us is our tarnished image abroad. The economic losses are already being expressed in concrete numbers. As always, such setbacks are coming at the wrong time. The economic boom is starting to slip, unemployment is on the rise, dangers from Eastern Europe are imminent—all in all, we Germans feel quite sorry for ourselves. We have worked so hard, attained such prosperity and such a good reputation as hard-working model boys, and now here we are, standing before the whole world in such a bad light. Do we deserve this?

And now another shock to our injured psyche: our showpiece of a country is already being compared to the rickety Germany that preceded the Nazi dictatorship. Can we no longer rely on the knowledge we have been accumulating over decades? Up until now, it has always been maintained that Bonn was not Weimar. Even now, the comparison is not a valid one, but perhaps it is at least a useful one. The fear that history could repeat itself, that a similarly devastating war could result, could bring the exasperated Germans in the East and in the West to reason.

There is good reason to doubt this, however. The expanded state of the unified Germans is behaving like a cornered animal. To protect itself from unfavorable changes, external as well as internal, stricter laws are being considered, instead of the existing laws being utilized to their fullest potential. But by following this course of action, the democratic constitutional state becomes its own worst enemy, and the right-wing radicals have every reason to gloat. A concession here, a concession there, and already our fine society is straying off course.

But does the private sector's stance not promise stabilization? Correct—in this case, it seems they can be relied upon, but their motives are not so much loftily idealistic as soundly profit-oriented. Products "made in Germany" are hard to sell on international markets when the rest of the world is observing the persecution of foreigners in Germany with such disgust.

Lady Di has already had to give back her Mercedes. It would be quite a blow if Germany's first-rate kitchen appliances were one day to become unsalable in the U.S. or anywhere else in the world. That would most likely mean the end of the patience toward the neo-Nazis. So, it looks like the prospects are good after all! The way the world economy is intermeshed these days, German industry will never stray onto the crooked path like they did under Adolf. But does that mean we are out of the woods?

No cry of outrage was raised throughout the country when German neo-Nazis forced a Jew to kneel and call out *"Sieg heil!"* The smugly lauded "liberal democratic order" *(freiheitlich demokratische Grundordnung)* is being crushed by the right-wing mob, and the nation is spinelessly submitting. Instead, the collective rage is being vented on the aliens, who are supposedly straining the social welfare system to the breaking point. Many politicians and the high-circulation press are trying their best, with reports about pseudo–asylum seekers, to provoke the population and to bring out the "eternally insulted Philistine" in the Germans. So much for the illusion that the lessons from the past had been learned once and for all.

"Germany for the Germans": up till now, only a few thousand have been screaming it, but the majority of Germans already agree with it.

It seems then that this country has lost all sense of reason, even though it is by no means suffering under conditions remotely like anything in the Weimar period. There is no economic crisis comparable to the one at that time, no fragmented, disunited political party scene, no festering wound of Versailles. On the contrary, our country was able to reunify (with outside help), is strong as an ox economically, and has a stable parliamentary system.

So why are the Germans so quick to fly off the handle? Perhaps Weimar does have a hand in this after all. The economic and political instability, and the resulting slide into dictatorship and war, have led to a hypertrophic-security mindedness in the Germans of today.

Encroachments of their security trigger abrupt defense mechanisms. Tolerance, which has never been one of the strengths of our people, did not exactly flourish under such circumstances. Another disadvantage is that we ourselves did not bring about our own democracy, but rather had it forced upon us, the vanquished opponents, by the Allied victors. This democracy was seen as a good system primarily for the reason that with a sufficiently disciplined approach, considerable affluence could and can be attained.

It was in this sense that the mammon-democracy a la West Germany was bequeathed to East Germany as well, or aspired to by the East Germans, as the case may be. As we know, the people in the former GDR were at first only demonstrating for freedom; they were not reckoning with reunification. It was not until later than the chant arose, "If the deutschmark doesn't come to us, we'll go to it." So it is no wonder that the same panic reactions are being observed in the East and in the West, ever since this consumer-oriented society has started to feel threatened by large numbers of immigrants.

It should not be surprising, then, that such a minor crisis should cause the pendulum to swing so far to the right. Such a phenomenon has already occurred, in the mid-1970s. At that time, the NPD* was gaining momentum, aided by economic problems. The media in this country went to great lengths to try and break the wave. The NPD was at first sharply attacked, then made to look ridiculous, then, as a last resort, ignored.

---

*An ultra-right-wing party.

But none of these tactics led to the desired success. The neo-Nazis were not stopped until the established parties fell in step and, after a transfer of power, offered an attractive foreign policy as well as economic success.

But no one seems to have much trust these days in the policies of the government or of the opposition. The major parties are looked upon as being incapable of solving problems. Right-wing radicalism is thus able to spread unchecked in Germany. What is more, the wrong approach has been used in bringing about German unity. Unification is seen primarily as an economic and financial policy operation, not as the bringing together of a cultural nation with intellectual and moral demands, and particularly with a responsibility toward the disadvantaged.

The unified Germans apparently cannot enjoy their unexpected good fortune. From the time of their joint beginnings they have found themselves in a state of emergency. Everything they experience, they perceive as undue stress. The people in the West fear for their material possessions; their fellow citizens in the East despair of being able to make the transition. Given this emotional state, whoever crosses their path, the asylum seekers for example, is treated as a menace. What this unstable society lacks are people with the moral stature of Heinrich Böll and Willy Brandt, whose vision and exemplary lives would have set convincing counterexamples to the neo-Nazis.

It looks again as though the media will not be able to handle the situation. They did not react quickly enough to the initial stage of the problems with the asylum seekers and the xenophobia. Media coverage of the acts of violence against foreigners has been accompanied by an underlying tone of stubborn conviction that things were not as bad as they seemed; the population is being constantly informed, but not enlightened. Attempts to shed light on the underlying causes have been at best sketchy. Civil courage crumbles quickly. For fear of violent right-wing radicals, local reporters leave the coverage of neo-Nazi excesses to out-of-town journalists.

Our society is putting up astonishingly little resistance. Instead, terms like "national crisis" and "national emergency" are cropping up surprisingly quickly. Instead of able-bodied democracy, we are experiencing helplessness on the part of the politicians and the press. To raise one's voice against the public menace of right-wing radicalism is a noble undertaking. But that alone cannot stop violence and xenophobia. Many exemplary actions are needed. But does our society have the necessary courage and moral consciousness? After the disgraceful beginning of the united Germany, proof of this has yet to be demonstrated.

Translated by Daniel Theisen

· 14 ·

ACCOUNTS OF CONDITIONS, FALL 1992

LEA ROSH

Hannover, Fall 1992

A disabled man rides his bike, his dog in front, his wife following, also on a bike and leaving distance between them. The man is an amputee, has lost his right leg in a car accident. His memory has also been affected; he was in a coma after the accident. He has struggled hard to regain a piece of normality. Once he had been a vital young man, athletic and muscular. Sports had been one of his passions. Of course that was over now. But being able to talk, walk, socialize—that he wanted to recapture. And it worked quite well, with time and according to the circumstances, as the attending physician attested.

Thus, a little bicycle trip along the roads of Grossburgwedel, district of Hannover. It is noon, school is over. Young people are walking towards the cyclist. Many young people. The wife of the disabled man recounts: First one of them had nudged her husband. She took it for an accident. But then more and more pushed him. They spat at him, spat at his face, his clothes, jeered at him: "You are living off our taxes," and, "Under Hitler they would have gassed you."

He rode on. His wife caught up. At a traffic light, on red, the students finally let go of their prey. The woman took him into an ice cream parlor. "We had to do something very ordinary and appealing, had to divert our thoughts." Only when she was cleaning him up in the bathroom, did she realize how badly he had been spat at, "from top to bottom."

The spat-at man could not divert his thoughts. The humiliation was too great. It was mortifying and degrading for him.

Two days later he was dead.

In his farewell letters, he told his wife, his doctor, and others, that this event had topped it all. It had not been new to him to be treated that way. In the stairway of a railway station he had once been jostled, the tires of his bike had been slashed. Jeering and jostling seemed to have been the order of the day.

An exceptional case?

Not at all.

Island of Spiekeroog, Summer 1992

A group of disabled people in wheelchairs used a paved beach path, easier for wheelchairs than going through sand. But the other tourists saw it completely differently. They reprimanded the disabled group. After all, *they* wanted to have *their* walks here. The disabled should see how they could get through the sand in their wheelchairs. "The paved path here, that's ours to walk on! The right of the stronger!"

Flensburg, Fall 1992

A judge finds for the plaintiffs in the case of German tourists claiming a 10 percent rebate of their travel expenses. The reason: In the breakfast room of their hotel, they had to suffer the sight of disabled people. "Sickening," the judge agreed, and he also attested to a "diminution of their recreation because of the sight." A 10 percent reimbursement of the travel expenses granted, of course.

"A life unworthy of living"? Whose life could possibly be unworthy, may we ask? Is it now once again the disabled people's turn, after it worked so well with the foreigners?

It did work quite well with the foreigners and the asylum seekers. Ten are dead, hundreds injured. Young girls maimed for life by burns. A man with both legs cut off by a train after he was drugged, chained, and put on the railway tracks. Rostock, Quedlinburg, Hünxe, Saarbruecken, Goettingen. . . . Where was the outcry? Where were the politicians, female or male, who as a group jointly went into the homes of the asylum seekers in order to make it clear to the right-wing mob that they would be there as protection?

Certainly. Hans-Jochen Vogel was in Leipzig. Richard von Weizäcker also went into a group home. And several others too. That is good. That is important. It sets an example. But it is not sufficient. Our lawful state remains silent. Our lawful state does not defend itself.

Sure, they were in Sachsenhausen. So what?

Waking up only when barracks of former Jewish prisoners are burning? The Jews of today are the others: The foreigners, the Turks, the Vietnamese, the Romany, the Sinti, the disabled. Sachsenhausen is a place we also have to go to if rioting occurs there. Yes. But in Rostock they set a home ablaze with about a hundred Vietnamese inside, fearing for their lives. And when the house was burning the police left. And the police did not protect the Vietnamese. Nor the courageous few who tried to protect those poor people and fought a battle with the skinheads in front of the building. The investigations of this scandalous event already have been going on for weeks. One has a foreboding of the outcome. One fears the outcome.

Quedlingburg, Fall 1992

Brawls. Evening after evening. Stones. Firebombs. The asylum seekers are finally transported elsewhere. The home is evacuated. And in a program of a public television station, the secretary of the interior of Sachsen-Anhalt, Hartmut Perschau [formerly in Hamburg] can explain the incident in the following way:

PERSCHAU: "In the beginning, on the first day, there were some right-wing scenes, and after that spectators and media worked each other up, which caused multiple police activity. We had the same spectacle every evening. Later on it was the kids, the local teens who had sought their evening entertainment and spectacle, and it was somewhat close to the limit of the tolerable. [He was not asked for whom intolerable.] At night we used to have almost more journalists at that asylants' home (!) than asylum seekers. There were sometimes fourteen television teams. Although none of the asylants was the slightest bit harmed. . . ."

MODERATOR: "We didn't drive the asylants (!) away."

PERSCHAU: "No . . . you know, forget about principles, if you organize that kind of a psychoterror there in front of a house for over a week. . . ."

MODERATOR: "Mr. Perschau, just to clarify this, it was not the television people who drove the asylants away, correct?"

PERSCHAU: "No, no. But obviously there is an interplay between spectators and the media because of course this is the place where these things too are always generated anew. When the police get involved, they have to clear the area of spectators and then, too, the cameras keep running. If you want to deescalate and not only escalate, then, at some point, you have to strictly interrupt certain things. Since then we have peace in Quedlinburg. And the opposition dared declare a victory of the right-wing extremists."

IGNATZ BUBIS (Central Council of the Jews in Germany): "But you don't have any asylants, you took them away, so of course you have peace now."

PERSCHAU: "As before, there is an asylant's home in Quedlinburg now. We did not give in, but it is simply not possible that we allow such spectacles to go unregimented. What happened there brought disrepute to Quedlinburg, disrepute to Sachsen-Anhalt and disrepute to Germany."

Soundtrack of a German secretary of the interior, secretary of Sachsen-Anhalt. No mentioning of those who really got harmed and hurt, the women and men who seek protection in our country. No word, and even worse, no thought of their fears, nightmares and anxieties, now and later on.

Our reputation is at stake.

No, much more is at stake.

Human rights, democracy, and our republic are at stake.

Now, this time, the democrats have to prevail in Germany. That is at stake. There have always been democrats in Germany even in 1914. Even in 1933. Even in 1938. Even 1939. But they were not strong enough. They succumbed. Is it going to happen again?

In the same television program, Heinrich Lummer could praise the party of the Republicans as a democratic party without being interrupted or stopped by anybody. Propaganda for the right, propaganda for brown. Finally lame, much too lame protests from Heide-Marie Wieczorek-Zeul. All others were silent.

We have long gotten used to it. Gotten used to it that politically misguided youths are allowed to speak up, that swastikas are being displayed, that the Hitler salute and right-wing slogans are being carried into our living rooms, that foreigners are being jeered, attacked, and killed. Gentleman's transgressions, quite clearly. To "smash a foreigner" may under certain circumstances cost no more than two years. Well, if that's how it is. . . .

Once again Hartmut Perschau, original soundtrack: "The mobilization of the street that we saw so often around these events, that is the real risk, this tinge of Weimar."

Wrong. The "tinge of Weimar" is the blindness for the right wing, the lack of action, the restraint.

What else has to happen?

Already so horribly much has happened: Ten people murdered. Close to two thousand assaults (up to October 25, 1992).

A disabled woman said: "I am afraid."

But another disabled person said: "I can understand that, but it's wrong. We have to learn to defend ourselves. And we will."

Translated by Sabine Tober

·15·

AN INCREDIBLE EVENT
(AN ANECDOTE)

KLAUS SCHLESINGER

In March 1975, thirty years after the collapse of German fascism, a Berlin university student, casually clad after the fashion of young intellectuals, with long hair and beard, returned from a visit by the Baltic sea with all the signs of psychic distress.

Because of a faulty wristwatch he had missed his train and was forced to make a stopover in A____, a district town in former Pomerania that had suffered a 70 percent destruction during the last war, and was inhabited by refugees from areas formerly belonging to the German Reich.

With two hours' time to spare, the student decided to have lunch in the railway station restaurant, which was half-empty, with only locals in it. Upon his entry he attracted everybody's glances, and was made the object of open and loud ridicule, the mildest of which was a comparison to Jesus in reference to his looks. Ignoring the ridicule, he sat down at a corner table, immersed himself in a newspaper, and hoped he would be soon forgotten by the people here. A misjudgment as it happened, for just a few minutes later, an obviously drunk man came to his table and questioned the student's cleaning habits in an openly sarcastic tone.

Young N., not wanting to be provoked, answered that he did not differ from other people in his cleaning habits, and asked to be left alone. Upon which the man spat out in front of him, and another man yelled from the background that he would not want to be touched by such an individuum if he were a woman.

Those present roared with laughter, and when the drunkard, still standing by the table, announced that he wanted to determine whether the beard of the strange guest was actually for real, the student jumped up from his chair and ran out of the restaurant, accompanied by derisive laughter.

Relieved, he entered the plaza in front of the station, which was empty and quiet on a Saturday, and began to walk through town. His feeling of relief, however, did not last long. Already the next locals he met, two workers painting a gate, could only shake their heads when they saw him. Some children who played ball on a meadow interrupted their game and pointed with fingers at him. When he wanted to change money at a newsstand to get coins for the telephone, the saleswoman snubbed him and shook her head, and whoever he met measured him in such a blatant way that it could only be characterized as punishment.

The student was so upset over this openly shown hostility that he could hardly look at the displays in the shop windows. Only one window he remembers very well. Part of the local photographer's shop, it displayed a considerable number of recent wedding pictures, presenting the couples in poses that evoked in the viewer spontaneous memories of photos from his grandmother's album.

From then on, he avoided the streets of the town. He passed the rest of his time on a marker by the highway, smoking. There he asked himself whether his observations could possibly have been overly tainted by that event in the railway station restaurant, enough to have caused him in his excited condition to read more into them than an incidental accumulation of non-characteristic events, or whether his very excitement made him realize something he otherwise might not have noticed.

He got an answer that very same hour. Thirty minutes before the departure of his train, he went onto the plaza in front of the station, and noticed an elderly man who stood with his back towards him, and who turned around when he heard the student's steps. The man, in his late sixties and of sturdy build, looked at the approaching student in astonishment, even bewilderment out of sunken eyes reddened by alcohol. He touched his head with his hand as if, unable to interpret the strange apparition, he was searching his memory for some lost image, and then, as if in sudden inspiration, he took a step forward, pointed at the student, and asked him in a loud voice, whether he was actually Jewish.

"Yes, you are a Jew," he continued, taking for assent the silence of the young man who sped up his steps, and then in an equally loud voice that he should hurry up and be gone.

"Get lost," he yelled after the fleeing student. "We're glad we got rid of you all."

Translated by Sabine Tober

·16·

OPEN SOCIETY AND ITS ENEMIES— MAKING A CASE AGAINST THE BRUTALIZATION OF THE REPUBLIC

THOMAS SCHMID

One of the advantages of the nowadays so-called old Federal Republic was that it gradually rendered traditional fascism superfluous. I have never felt particularly comfortable in the company of antifascists. In their speeches I disliked the tinge of a holier-than-thou attitude, so common in the GDR; I distrusted their Manichaeism separating the world neatly into good and evil, and their unwillingness to acknowledge the existence of the Federal Republic annoyed me most of all. Each and every isolated little group that employed radical right-wing insignia was welcome proof for them that in fact nothing had changed despite all that democratic varnish. Lecherously, they quoted again and again the metaphor of the still fertile womb, and one could not avoid getting the impression that many antifascists were in desperate need of the few existing nazis so they could hold on to their cherished image of the world, or, rather, of Germany.

It used to be easy to stay away from such company. Over a long period of time the Republic has proven to be extremely stable. No ambitions whatsoever of becoming a superpower—on the contrary, contentment rather in the blind spot of history. Democracy itself, which many politicians of the first hour still saw as an apparatus, was adopted by later dissenting generations. Political struggles gradually lost their antagonistic drift. Not enemies, but opponents fought each other, and the consensus about the common good being worth keeping grew. This Republic has often been reproached for being unpretentious and for rejecting any radical alternation of courses. But both these are also an expression of an understanding that is invaluable against the background of German history, namely, that peace within society is a higher good than the truths of struggling parties. The Federal Republic of Germany began slowly to adopt the pragmatic Anglo-Saxon image of democracy, according to which the rules and procedures are more important than any of the given contents. And we could be reasonably convinced that in cases of doubt and crisis the political class in its majority would stand by these foundations of the Republic.

We cannot be sure of that any more, and, in that respect, the eternal antifascists were proven right. As if one needed yet another testimony that this Republic is not the "old one" any more, Rostock-Lichtenhagen and its consequences provided just that. For the first time, arsonists, by coincidence only saved from being murderers, were able to carry their acts out with the mental and moral support of large segments of the population. As never before, for moments, almost for days, the state's monopoly on power was suspended. There are situations when siding with the victim is the only thing that counts. Here was such a situation. What happened instead? Of course, they all went on record expressing their disgust, and then, from Rudolf Seiters to Bjoern Engholm, in the very next sentence, they claimed that a change of Article 16 of the Constitution was more urgently necessary now than ever. All those who talked that way basically vindicated the arsonists. These people did *not* make a stand, they did *not* give priority to the rules, and they did *not* make a strong case for the common democratic cause vis-à-vis the foes of democracy.

In a given democracy that for good reasons is representative and indirect, politicians do not execute the will of the people. Although it is their task to react to moods in interests of the population, it is not their task to yield to such moods and interests for the mere reason that they exist. However, that exactly is what sizeable parts of the political class did: they surrendered their autonomy. The arsonists are herding them.

What would have been advisable after Hoyerswerda and Huenxe, was made imperative by Rostock-Lichtenhagen: a moratorium in the question of the asylum laws. The political class ought to have had the sensitivity and the resolve to make one thing clear beyond any doubt: while it is true that in a democracy everything can be discussed and negotiated, this can never ever be done under pressure from the mob. A political class that does so nonetheless surrenders its power.

We must acknowledge today that the Federal Republic is about to fail the first real test of his history. As even those who doggedly pursue the changes of Article 16 well know, this test has relatively little to do with the institution of asylum or the actual numbers of asylum seekers. What is happening once again, is that Germany cannot come to terms with itself, that it is leaderless in its reaction to its own unification as well as to the new world disorder, which, for now irrevocably, brings an end to the times of contentment in the blind spot. After the end of the bloc confrontation, politics cannot be anything else but a game with relatively many unknowns, a game where the old Federal virtues of resolve and moderation would be needed more than ever. But instead of going along with this difficult process, in Germany one leans towards a flight into a phantom debate over the question of asylum, just as if smaller numbers of asylum seekers would even slightly change the problems confronting the country that became sovereign in such an unsovereign way.

So what is to be done? The first point of order is to counteract decisively the brutalization of the East. More than fifty years of dictatorial continuity have nourished the misconception on the territory of the former GDR that freedom gives you among other things and perhaps most of all the right finally to let it all hang out. It is not astonishing that older and more authoritarian mentalities have survived in this part of Germany that has re-mained German in such an antiquated way. Nothing, however, would be less appropriate than showing an understanding that, in consideration of the economic and social misery in the new states, is fed by a bad conscience (which especially Social Demo-cratic politicians are prone to). Misery is no excuse for crude-ness. The civilization of the East with all possible means is urgently required, especially so in face of the danger that the new misery-born chauvinism might taint Western Germany too, stronger than before.

Secondly, we finally must focus in the debate on a fact that was only disguised by the arguing over asylum, namely the fact that Germany is now and will remain an immigration country. Rather than having chimeric disputes over how to undo this decades-long, yet stubbornly denied reality, we need to adjust the institutional apparatus of the Federal Republic to it. There is no doubt about it, immigration creates problems. But an immigration that is being denied, despite its very existence, creates even bigger problems. It is not truth itself but rather its denial that is hard to digest. We must spell out what everybody basically already knows, that Germany cannot stay apart from the shifting that is a necessary consequence of the ending East-West bloc confrontation. Germany will continue to rely on immigration, which incidentally helps rather than hurts, and it will not be able to fend it off by democratic means. As a civilized country, it will not be able to rid itself of its self-imposed obligation to accept refugees. And it would be well advised to abandon its last nationalistic definition of citizenship, namely that being German means being of German blood.

Thirdly, we ought to avoid countering the right-wing national hysteria with an antifascist hysteria. The fact that the political class largely gave in, does not imply that society as a whole will do likewise. There is a relatively stable civil consciousness in the "old" Federal Republic that, quite differently from 1932, reaches far into circles of industry. At the core of this civil self-awareness is the conviction that conflicts must be solved in principle by peaceful means, and that this Republic shall be open to the world. Gone are the days when one could assume that such a conviction was common to the political class as a whole. Therefore, it is now up to society to make itself clearly heard, to remind the political class of its justification for doing business, and to confront authoritatively the arsonists who today set the tone. All those who are not only appalled by this rampantly expressed xenophobia, but who also feel that their own quality of life is diminished by it, should now bring to bear the impact of their experiences and of their fondness for this Republic. It might prove to be true then that democracy in Germany has many more followers than the antifascists fear, and the arsonists hope.

Translated by Sabine Tober

·17·

FROM THE SPEECH AT FRANKFURT'S PAULSKIRCHE

HELMUT SCHMIDT

Why do we tolerate a situation in which the foreigners living in our midst, as well as our European neighbors and ourselves, are stricken with fear by the ever-increasing number of reprehensible xenophobic violent crimes? In some neighborhoods the problem is not only one of mere passivity on the part of nonparticipating citizens, but unfortunately one of secret approval as well—a moral scandal! And in several of our large cities, we have, in the meantime, more than a thousand youths prone to violence; left extremists as well as right extremists are at the point of developing super-regional organization; the perpetrators in Rostock, for example, came in part from the West.

We fought the murderous Baader-Meinhof terrorists with high constitutional severity and with fundamental determination; Mogadishu was the high point of this struggle. Today we must proceed with the same determination against violent right extremists: the police and the courts must enable speedy apprehension, a quick trial and an immediate execution of sentence.

At the time of Mogadishu, the moral-religious leadership, with the assistance of the politicians of all the parties, had enhanced the peoples' contempt for the RAF. These days any claim to moral-religious leadership appears to have gone bankrupt. If, however, we should find ourselves unable to handle the skinheads, the neo-Nazis and the self-described "autonomous" perpetrators of violence in time, then all of us Germans will be the worse for it.

To the youth who neither recognize nor wish to recognize any authority, the current flow of foreigners into Germany is a welcome opportunity to vent their frustration. The one group attacks foreigners, the other attacks the attackers, both groups are prepared for violence, and still others are allowing themselves to be taken in. By grouping all foreigners in the same category, far too many adults are, in fact, being taken in as well. Unfortunately, no one is telling them that the millions of foreigners who have for many years now worked and resided in our midst are no less law-abiding than German citizens. When, however, in 1992 alone their ranks are augmented by almost one-half million newcomers for whom there are neither living quarters nor jobs, then all suffer for it: both the Germans fearing for their own jobs as well as the long socially assimilated foreign guests of many years. And this is not to mention the new arrivals who suffer under an uncertain future.

Many of the new arrivals would like to come to Germany because they have the hope that, economically and socially, their lives will be better here than at home. They therefore maintain, contrary to the truth, that they were politically perse-cuted at home and ought therefore be granted asylum in the spirit of Article 16 of our Basic Law.

I am of the firm moral conviction that we must continue to grant asylum to those truly politically persecuted in their own homeland. This is one moral principle which we ought not assail.

By no means, however, does our present-day Article 16 of the Constitution require that we continue to accept up to a half-million foreigners every year. By no means does it require that the asylum-review procedure drag on for months and years (there are to date over 350,000 old, unsettled petitions for asy-lum!). It also does not require that full social assistance be provided the applicants. We need, rather, on a nationwide basis, modest room and board for the duration of the review proce-dure. We need an unequivocal, efficient deportation procedure in place for all those cases for which applications have been turned down—especially where political persecution has been merely feigned—or where the applicant has been criminally li-able, for instance through the dealing of drugs. Our previous laws, created for far different times, require decisive renovation and speedy, practical administration.

The debate by politicians concerning Article 16 has not yet revealed how they plan to deal with the problem on a practical level. Even if we assume that parliament will amend Article 16, we are nonetheless left in the dark as to how the coalition and the opposition plan to proceed practically. Both should finally show their true colors! They must cease their mutual defama-tion campaigns and finally put foward viable, legal proposals. Using clear distinctions between politically persecuted for-eigners, refugees from foreign and civil wars, immigrants of German ethnic origin and, ultimately, all the different types of people wishing to immigrate, they must prescribe a quick appropriate procedure for each of these groups.

The public has a right to be informed and to judge how those in the government intend to solve this complex of problems. Lacking that, the anger and fear will simply escalate.

Translated by Martin Black

·18·

ABOUT THE ORIGINS OF RIGHTIST YOUTH BRUTALITY IN GERMANY

WOLFGANG THIERSE

One cannot help using the terms "racist" and "fascist" for the brutal excesses against foreigners in Germany. Nonetheless, caution is needed, because the perpetrators are not always youths with a clearly determined ideological orientation. Often they are disoriented and frightened children, stigmatizing whom would render dialogues impossible. If I recommend the use of the labels "racist" and "fascist" anyhow, I am doing that because aggressive, latently brutal, and authoritarian ways of thinking and acting are gradually intertwined with primitive piece work of a fascist-racist ideology. The more influence the radical right-wing travel cadres gain over these children and youths out of control, the greater is the danger that the so far anarchic, fright-propelled, in the final analysis even helpless use of force will by and by acquire a dubious, subjective meaning that in turn could cause further escalation.

The first pedagogically guided step in the drive against right-wing youth brutality is therefore a discriminating way of observing it, followed by differentiated modes of action.

The pugnacious youths are not just *Schmuddelkinder* on the fringes, outlaws without any chances in a new social order that many East Germans see as being merciless; children who in despair scream for attention and affection. Thoughtless, xenophobic Sunday chats in the living rooms of "good citizens" provide a background, and, even worse, whatever angry resignation fathers (and mothers) articulate and hold back at home, their children express publicly in the language of force.

The causes seem self-evident: A GDR society, tight, isolated, even walled-in and seemingly self-sufficient, lost overnight its cohesion, which up to this point had been kept intact by means of all kinds of force and pressure. The unification process started an upheaval of learned and practiced modes of conduct. The principles of state, society, and individual, as taught by "Real Existing Socialism," have collapsed, and that shakes up the handed-down, yes, *preserved* experiences in everybody. The inherited values and norms erode; what once was reliable and binding, dissolves. What was right before, proves to be, or is declared wrong now. The dread of a straight social decline, the fear of not being able to escape an existence in the social shadow of the united Germany, these are underlying motives throwing light on the brutality against the weakest of the weak, although by no means condoning it. A conflict originally social is being waged on the backs of foreigners, and thus is turning ethnic.

Although there are specifically East German causes for the racist excesses, right-wing extremism is not an exclusively East German phenomenon. It is gaining ground in the West German states as well as outside of Germany. The creeping ethnicization of social conflicts is a challenge for all of Europe. But the vehemence with which the radical force gained ground particularly in East Germany in the past months, leads to the question of the special conditions and mechanisms that explain the eruptive, direct, and "spontaneous" character of rightist brutality. (For radical right-wing and nationalistic attitudes are not more common in the East than in the West. As all the polls indicate, rather the opposite is the case.)

Intellect and emotions cannot keep up with the speed and totality of the change of social systems. The open society based on competition demands such a high level of individuality, self-representation, and competitiveness, that the average GDR citizen, just released from state tutelage, must feel overwhelmed. There is neither place nor time left for people to make sure of what is theirs and has become so uncertain: How much of the learned knowledge is still valid, of the grown experiences, and the enforced codes of behavior? There is a new vacuum of meaning now, and the radical right is gradually and creepingly starting to fill that vacuum with its banal-brutal interpretation of reality.

The catastrophic economic and social situation causes, hones, and prolongs the state of disorientation. The loss of jobs and the decline in industrial production since 1989 are turning East Germany into a dying industrial region. Existential anxieties and the loss of everything that had been reliable for years, wear people's identity down and gradually destroy their self-esteem. The economic and social determinants require a rich pool of individual problem-solving abilities, of ways of coping with these thus far unknown anxieties and burgeoning aggressions, of coping mechanisms that help avoid a turn into destruction and keep people from being seduced by the simplistic answers of ideological rooks. The Germans in the GDR had no or very little opportunity to learn such coping mechanisms.

The party-run state tried to create a homogeneous society by means of nationalistic, patriotic appeals to the population (in its beginning) and militancy in its educational system (in its later years). The creation of an own state identity was attempted among other things by means of a physical separation from the outside world, and a hostility towards everything foreign and different. A simplifying image of the world, which, goal-oriented and with demagogic slogans, cut down on the complexity of economic, social, and cultural processes, consequently produced simplistic, single-cause explanations of "world" and "me," good and evil, right and wrong. Citizens of the GDR did not have the chance to test the limitations of their tolerance, and to gain intercultural, enriching experiences. Solution-oriented dealing with complex conflicts of interest, peaceful conflict solution was not part of the repertoire of "real socialist" curricula. Social crises, in particular those involving hardships for the citizens had no place in the Marxist-Leninist vision of their own, so-called harmonious society. The "Capitalist-Imperialist" foreign countries were the declared designers of grim circumstances, and responsibility was thus delegated to the outside. The fault was always with the others.

In the present, extremely problematic socioeconomic situation, strangers, foreigners, asylum seekers, and asylants appear as dangers and must be fended off. Almost as before, identity is being created or stabilized by means of separation, of hostility against all that is foreign and different. Individual living arrangements (formerly social arrangements) are secured and legitimized by a rigorous rejection of the practices (formerly social systems) of others. This mental pattern is widely used—not just in this context, and, God knows, not just in East Germany. Everybody adopting this pattern will unavoidably find out that this is not the way to gain anything close to a positive, genuinely stable self-confidence. One's own lot does not improve through a declaration of the others' as being even worse and inferior, and, above all, an identity created by means of separation remains extremely fragile, and thus needs to be protected rather aggressively.

Once again, we must examine and consider the GDR's past in order to find out why it is in East Germany that the overt barrage of frustration and the widespread disorientation find their expression in right-wing orgies of brutality, mainly staged by youths. Party-line antifascism and internationalism used to be authoritatively decreed government doctrines. The use of fascist symbols and the adoption of smooth simplistic elements of fascist ideology appear as the strongest form of rejection of the past social order as well as of that being shaped today. Since neither Socialism nor Capitalism dealt or deal with the needs of the young in desirable ways, fascistoid "solutions" suddenly appear as plausible alternatives. After a time of hope kindled by many predictions and promises, the disappointment is just the greater in the face of an increasing economic and social depression and the daily repeated experience of individual powerlessness in a democratic society. Young people find themselves still and again pawns in a murky yet powerful process, in which they cannot actively participate.

The common feeling of disadvantage next to the West, the clearly inferior living conditions, and the immanent irrelevance of life itself, they all need a forum, a platform for self-expression. If politics does not provide such a forum for dissatisfaction to be aired "upward" and trigger consequences, dissatisfaction will turn "downward" against those weaker and weakest, against the minorities of society. Foreigners and asylum seekers function only as one possible target of the outburst, other social and cultural groups on the fringes might be targeted equally as well. If the politicians, however, as a reaction to the outbursts, recognize the existence of an urgent asylants' problem, the pug-

nacious youths are indirectly provided with a political justification. Force brings about results, their "voice" is being heard,
politicians react in the desired manner, the first step from impo-
tant object to potent subject seems thus successfully taken.

The enlightened contemporary, however, knows that the real
problem has nothing to do with foreigners, but rather with
ourselves, with our commonly plain way of dealing with conflict, with our social and political organizations, and our
blurred view of reality. It seems to be enormously difficult for
us, however, to see things this way, and not only for those of
us who use force. But, since foreigners are neither the cause nor
the only possible target group of potential eruptions of hatred,
politicians must not settle on "the question of the foreigners"
or "the asylants' problem." Brutality will not go away once
the foreigners are gone. *The problem of people from outside
Germany is above all a problem of people from inside
Germany.*

Our level of tolerance in thought and action depends on how
well we manage to distance ourselves from the familiar and
turn to the unfamiliar. It also depends on whether our self-
confidence allows us not to see as dangerous what is alien to
us, but rather experience it as a gain and supplement. If that
fails, everybody different, foreigners, the other gender, Jews,
homosexuals, are discriminated against as deviants. Intolerance
is the direct consequence of a negatively construed identity that
needs to look constantly to the outside, debase what is different,
and thereby be assured of its own quality of life. The end of
the Cold War, and the reconstruction of a unified German national state abolished the outside enemy in East and West, and
by that very act liberated so far tied-up anxieties and loosened
relatively stable circumstances: Thus, all those whose psychological equilibrium was based on the existence of outside ene-

mies and black-and-white imagery, must now find new enemy representations. . . .

Right-wing extremism increasingly reflects and represents our social interactions and interrelations as well as our political understanding, and that even more so than we like to admit at this point. It is not just a deviantly malicious phenomenon that counteracts social development. It flushes the sediments and the backwash of social decay to the surface. Right-wing extremism does not employ programs. It offers smooth messages which require neither the painstaking use of reason nor any kind of critical independent thinking, messages that are readily duplicated. It is the dangerous street song of the political world.

Politicians and society as a whole must admit that they did not in time recognize the first signs of this nasty development. Irrespective of whether a gradual dissolving of radical right-wing potentials is possible, from now on we need to develop early warning systems that alert us in time. Politics and society must become more transparent and accessible. The representative character of political democracy must be softened. Politics must not give in to populisms. But the sentiments of the population and the sensitivity of politicians must correspond. Political communication is impossible once the connection between sender and recipient is disrupted. Politicians must be sensitive to the populace without giving in to their every whim!

In the short term, it is correct and understood that the lawful state must protect its foreign-born citizens from acts of brutality. Among other things, it is thus crucial to make the police machinery more effective as to avoid such scandalous events as those recently in Rostock. Above all, it is essential that political and social forces, united by a consensus still to be found, draw clearly discernible limits. This has to be clear to everyone: A new fascism will not only be intolerable, but indeed actively and persistently combated. The stigmatizing of brute force and fascist ideology, however, is different from the criminalization of children and teens. For, in the long run, rioting with its roots in penetrating experiences of dissolving solidarity, disorientation, and powerlessness will not be avoided through the use of state force. A reliable reconciliation will be achieved only with the creation of social networks. This task is certainly too much for the state by itself, but the state can and must provide the framework.

It is only on a secure social basis that a moral and civilized stability will be achieved and maintained. So far, the East Germans have got only undeveloped chances for social partnership. As long as the social context appears as an undefined, frightening chaos, what remains out of personal reach, are decent salaries and professional growth as well as stable and reliable social contexts that could serve as bases for new identifications, and not just those that stem from being German.

Translated by Sabine Tober

·19·

UNIFICATION IN CRISIS

HEINRICH-AUGUST WINKLER

Two years after the German unification, Germany finds itself in a unification crisis. One of the causes, or rather, one whole bundle of causes is quite obvious: Whereas the making of a unified state was a masterpiece of foreign politics, it was a poor job of national politics. The most weighty inherent flaw of the unification contract, the principle of "return of property before compensation of former proprietors," constitutes now as before a main obstacle to an "upswing in the East," and the responsibility of the contract's architects for this is not diminished by the fact that they do not have to take the blame for yet another big barrier to economic development in the new Federal States, namely the collapse of the former GDR's Eastern markets.

Also clearly "homemade" is yet another drawback of the unification process: The disastrous misjudgements of its costs, and the chancellor's failure to prepare West and East Germans for the troubles of the years to come at the psychologically appropriate time, namely before the unification.

There was even more wrong-track switching in 1990. But that does not suffice to explain the crisis in which Germany finds itself in the fall of 1992. What we witness today is rather mainly a consequence of the separate development and alienation that took place during four decades of national separation of (East) Germans and (West) Germans.

German unification came unexpected. Until this fall, there were only a few people in the former Federal Republic who still believed in the restitution of German unity. Whenever "reunification" was conjured up in the West during the seventies and eighties, it was mostly to suit West German political goals—the recovery of right-wing voter groups, and the fight against opponents left of center. Most Social Democrats considered lip service for national unity counterproductive: The other German state ought not to be threatened with abolishment, if change for the better in the GDR was to be achieved, change towards more freedom, and thereby more common ground with the Federal Republic. A portion of the left went further, and did not only say no to a national German state, but also to the idea of a German nation.

In the GDR up to the very end, hopes for German unity were wider spread and deeper rooted than in the West. Civil rights activists, however, in their majority did even beyond the "turning point" of fall 1989 not aim at a unification with the Federal Republic, but at the persistent democratization of the GDR. The "peaceful revolution" began under the banner of the slogan "We are the people." The call "We are *one* people" could only be heard once the collapse of GDR power was in full swing, and Soviet intervention was no longer a danger.

The call for unity was popular with the masses because it implied what the majority of East Germans wanted to express. In negative terms that was their rejection of the failed system of "real existing Socialism" as well as of any attempts of reforms of this system, or of finding a "third" way between Capitalism and Communism. And in positive terms, it was their claim for material equality with the privileged Germans of the Federal Republic.

The Federal Republic had to accept what the majority of East Germans wanted. It had to do so not only because it was bound to by the preamble to the constitution and the Supreme Court's decision on the Contract of Basic Stipulations of 1973. It had to do so also for an ethical reason: From an inner-German viewpoint, the Germans in the GDR were the real losers of World War II. They had paid a considerably higher price than the West Germans for the National-Socialist regime.

Forcing upon the East Germans a GDR that they did not want, and which the Soviet Union no longer insisted upon, to see that as an alternative to unification, is a viewpoint that was and must be left to some left-wing disciples of Metternich.

The unification crisis is a consequence not only of an enormous economic discrepancy between West and East Germany, but also of the clash of extremely different worlds of experience. In the old Federal Republic, a "post national" consciousness had gradually developed. The integration into the West had been internalized in its cultural aspects also by many who had bitterly fought the politics of the first chancellor. Posthumous Adenauer left-wingers are among those strongly advocating a preservation of what Juergen Habermas in 1986 called the one great intellectual achievement of the postwar era, the "unconditional opening of the Federal Republic to the political culture of the West."

In the GDR, this process of Westernization could occur neither in the political nor in the everyday culture. Many observers therefore saw the smaller of the two German states as being more "German" than the larger one. Other than in the old Federal Republic, in East Germany there were also hardly any possibilities to get used to living with foreigners. Here is one of the reasons for the more open xenophobia in the new federal states as opposed to the old ones. In addition, there is the feeling of constantly getting the short end of the stick vis-à-vis the "Wessies." And in some of the new citizens of the Federal Republic, this creates the need to prove themselves as particularly good Germans: through aggressive behavior towards foreigners and especially the socially weakest among them.

The GDR considered itself an antifascist state. But a state-decreed antifascism, hardened into formulas, did, in considerable parts of the younger generation, further neither an understanding of history nor of moral sensitivity, but rather of stubbornness. In the later days of the GDR, there was already a neo-Nazi youth movement, though the public knew almost nothing about it. Today, the open display of NS symbols may often be just an intentional provocation, a provocation that, according to Peter Merseburger, aims at two different targets: the former pillars of the Communist regime on the one hand, and the new democratic state on the other. But next to that, there is also, and not only among the youth, a reservoir of true right-wing radicalism, and we do not yet know whether it is larger in the new or the old federal states.

In East as well as West Germany, asylum seekers constitute the preferred targets of young rioters. They take advantage of a widespread fear of a mass influx from the poor countries of Eastern Europe and the "Third World." Such a fear is not unfounded. No democratic party can afford to ignore it or talk it away. The asylum article of the Constitution raises hopes that Germany cannot fulfill. It was formulated at a time when nobody could imagine any economically caused mass influx into Germany. We need an amendment to Article 16, guaranteeing an individual right to political asylum, yet countering any abuse of it. Otherwise, we might face a hopeless polarization of the democratic parties. The forces of the extreme right would triumph, and the right to asylum together with German democracy would lose out.

The amendment to Article 16 is only part of the problem. Germany must part with that basic myth of not being an immigration country. That claim cannot be sustained in face of the economic and demographic reality: Germany needs immigrants. An immigration law with quota regulations is therefore overdue. The rights of permanent resident aliens in Germany must be strengthened, and the acquisition of citizenship must be made easier for them, and even more so for their children born in Germany. But, in both areas, immigration and asylum, German efforts alone cannot suffice. Only a united Europe can successfully meet the challenges that, at least largely, originate in the global prosperity slope.

Even without the German unification of 1990, asylum and immigration would be debated topics in (Federal) German politics. But the disappearance of the Iron Curtain has made both these problem areas more acute or, to put it differently, has caused a change from quantity to quality. For the former Federal Republic, the wall had been a protective wall, a safeguard against global problems, the severity of which the Germans are only now beginning to grasp. The wall was, however, an "antifascist rampart" only insofar as it sheltered the Federal Republic up to 1989 from fascism produced by the GDR itself.

Yet another presently acute point of contention, the issue of United Nations combat availability of the Bundeswehr, would be discussed today, even if there was no united Germany. But here, too, it is true that the problem has gained new dimensions because of the events of 1989–90, and that it has acquired a different quality because of the increase in political weight that came with the unification. Changes in the Constitution are unavoidable. Germany cannot indefinitely claim a special role for itself that is too comfortable to be ethically convincing. Macabre indeed is an assertion frequently made by some members of the left, namely that the experiences of the National-Socialist era and World War II oblige Germany to under no circumstances give military assistance to the United Nations in its actions against breaches of international law. Neutral positions in questions of right and wrong cannot possibly be the quintessence of what we can learn from the years 1933 to 1945.

The former Federal Republic was everything but consistent in its efforts to "come to terms" with its National-Socialist past. The swelling of the nonparliamentary opposition by members of the academic youth in the second half of the sixties was caused primarily by the then well-founded criticism that in the Federal Republic the Nazi era had been repressed rather than rationally worked through. Despite all the differences between the two German dictatorships, the National-Socialist and the SED (GDR state party) one: If the demand in the former GDR for letting bygones be bygones should prevail, the consequences would in some respects compare to the collective acts of repression after 1945. Sooner or later, we would have to pay for it, though this time to the right, and not, as in 1968, to the left.

The unification crisis is not over. There is no reason for either fatalism or else a hasty all-clear signal. The former Federal Republic has dealt successfully with basically similar turmoils in the second half of the sixties, and has come out even stronger. At that time, too, the causative factors of the crisis were mainly economic, and one of the most visible political alarm indicators were horrendous gains of a right wing party, the NDP. Its attraction was diminished as soon as the democratic system proved that it was not just good for fair-weather periods.

Such a proof is needed today also, during the first great challenge of the united Germany's democracy.

Translated by Sabine Tober

·20·

WORLD MUSIC

HANS ZENDER

The essence of art is not only seismographic or utopian: it does not only tell of future catastrophies or times of bliss; art is also a reflection of the reality of the present. Like an X ray, it reveals to those capable of reading it, whatever viable trends have developed within a given society.

Twentieth-century art in its entity testifies that human life has entered irreversibly into a global, and thereby necessarily multicultural era. It makes us proud that the Federal Republic of Germany after World War II has made a unique contribution here, and we fail to understand how it is possible that in the very same republic overt and covert signs of the old barbarism are surfacing, as if grown historical structures could be undone without causing the most severe damage.

Great art cannot lie. Once manipulated by the ruling forces, it reacts with sterility and death. Neither Hitler's, nor Stalin's, nor Mao's empires have come up with one single viable piece of art, despite all the efforts made in that direction. Officially decreed folklore as an indicator of closeness to the people, and enforced ties between art and national traditions nipped creativity in the bud, and ruined great talents (as for example Shostakovich).

Hardly any of the great artworks that originated in the course of this century in the free part of the world can still be solely understood from within the world of its creator's national origin. An unstoppable interaction and mutual influence has begun between previously clearly separated traditions. Of course, there were great historic eras during which great art could originate from national enthusiasm. As a last, almost already nostalgic wave, the national schools of the history of music of the nineteenth century (reaching into the first half of the twentieth), give testimony of at least the strength of national movements of the time. With the beginning of the modern, however, these trends disappeared from the spectrum of music. In its place, there are on the one hand a free, quasi-abstract music, void of all folkloristic colorations, on the other hand an abundance of works combining the "folklores" of different cultures. As John Cage wrote to me just a few weeks before his death about one of his main pieces ("Renga Plus Apartment House"), he wanted to present with this composition a portrait of his American country and its inherent multicultural structure: It combines chorals, dances, and marches of the immigrants with American Indian chants, Negro songs, and those of Sephardic Jews and Quakers. And Cage's spiritual antidode, Oliver Messiaen, made his inspirational idea of a type of Catholicism embracing all the cultures of the world, concrete in his own way by assembling the multilayered style of his mammoth work from (individually clearly traceable) French, German, Russian, Indian-Hindu, Balinese, Peruvian, and ancient Greek components, not to mention the Gregorian chant that by itself is already a combination product of early Christian syncretism.

It might not be accidental that the idea of a "world music" was formulated for the first time in Germany in the middle of this century. After all, it was here that at Goethe's time the terms of *world literature* and *World Citizenship* were coined. The Stockhausen of hymns and telemusic quite habitually thinks multiculturally. Bernd Alois Zimmermann expands this thought to the idea of a "pluralistic music," which assumes that in modern consciousness there is a simultaneous presence of all national heritages as well as of all historical eras. Such aesthetics is, so to speak, an incarnation of tolerance; this message can be understood without any further substantial statements.

After World War II, it was undoubtedly in the Federal Republic that the encounter of composers from not only all of Europe, but also the Americas and Asia took place, an encounter of unprecedented richness in the history of music. Practically all of the then young composers began their careers here, or else received substantial support here: Pierre Boulez, Luigi Nono, Bruno Maderna, Luciano Berio, Mauricio Kagel, Gyoergy Ligeti, Isang Yun—just to mention the most renowned names; but also the Americans, Cage, Feldman, Brown, have built up so much influence here that even today, they find larger audiences here than in the U.S.A. In the melting pots of the courses at Darmstadt, the music festivals at Donaueschingen, and the large series for new music on German radio stations, there was in complete tolerance and infinite diversity a rich harvest that raised German musical life, at least in respect to new music, to world levels.

Many of the just-named composers stayed in the Federal Republic of Germany; and a similar picture could be seen with singers, soloists, and conductors, so that today musicians internationally meet actually like members of a big family. The German orchestras, seemingly damaged beyond repair by the expulsion of Jewish musicians, have also been able to gradually improve their level of performance with the help of a large proportion of foreign musicians. (Hindemith still said to me in 1960 when I assisted him: "The German orchestras will never recover from the loss of the Jewish musicians!") Looking now at the all new ensemble scene, so important for the new music: in its most prominent group, the "ensemble modern," as many German and foreign players perform together. It becomes also obvious here that the reason for this development is not just a lack of good German musicians, but above all the unique creative spirit that comes with the combination of equally gifted artists from various cultural backgrounds who are well tuned into each other. Only that can bring about an art of such complexity as to do justice to today's world. Science and technology, economics and politics have presented us with a world that is intertwined, and ever more so, and it is up to the arts to find ways of giving this world a new character and spirit.

And now we are sitting day after day shocked anew in front of the evening news, hearing of attacks on asylants, desecration of cemeteries, and neo-Nazi activity. . . . One thinks one is dreaming when one hears of the lukewarm reactions of some politicians, and listens as some members of parties with a "C" in their emblem seriously question the evidence of a multicultural structure in a modern society. Those who beat up and burn down, probably cannot see what it really is they are doing, and how they damage most what they believe to "fight for." But our hair stands up when we ask ourselves how something like this can happen towards the end of this century. Do late consequences of Germany's collective maladies during the past decades now suddenly surface after all? Has the spiritual essence of the Germans been damaged at root level by first, twelve years of stultification through the craze of nazism, and then, forty years of stultification through the so-called Marxist-Leninism on the one side and the complete spiritual void of the department-store and growth ideology on the other side? Has our society, have its cultural institutions failed in passing on a meaning of culture that does not only imply knowledge and order, but above all compassion and tolerance?

Were I a man of the church, or else an educator, my despair would be complete. As a scientist, I would be once again deeply troubled over the old question: Has scientific thinking become so closely intertwined with technology and economics that it turned from a blossoming of the human spirit to a manifestation of manipulating forces that breed egotism instead of creating more humaneness? As an artist, I have to ask myself whether our cultural life has not sunk to the level of an entertainment industry, primarily economically oriented, and enginelike despite its loudly maintained intellectual claim. As has happened never before, the art of past centuries is being cannibalized and abused: by some for purposes of representation and self celebration, (in quite unjustified identification with a "value world" that we can hardly understand any more), by others for purposes of career advancement, self-representation, and financial security. Whoever services the institutions and media unthinkingly becomes guilty of just that thoughtless deprivation of culture of all direct humaneness, guilty of debasing works of art for educational or entertainment purposes. "It comes from the heart—let it reach the heart," that is what Beethoven wrote on one of his last scores. But what does that mean? "Heart," that is that innermost meeting place of structure and affectation, of interior and exterior. The reception of culture in our society is increasingly in danger of paying attention to just the glittering surface and the appearance of art that can be rationally analyzed; Culture thus loses its humane responsibility, and turns into an empty phrase. This is rather difficult to avoid, for the fate of all anarchists, namely sterility, destructiveness, and eventually ineffectiveness, threatens those who stand up against the ruling institutions. It may well be necessary to find a way in between all the institutional structures, and thus a true independence capable of articulating itself from within as well as outside the institutions.

Democracy in Germany faces a great challenge. During the past period of fair weather democracy, a noncommittal understanding of culture could seem to be sufficient, one that yielded to the taste of the majority.

In this situation, we should see an opportunity to look for a new sincerity: It is critical that we present the great messages of art, and in particular the signals of modern art more powerfully and vividly. How? With verbal interpretations? That would land us either in academia or the back pages of the newspapers. Through explicitly formulated political contents, or else through its symbolic codification within certain formal systems? Both ways have been used to their full extend. Left-wing slogans do not help, and neither do lamentations over Armageddon. What we have to do is accept the Modern in all its difficult complexity, finally open it up to a broader public, decode its spiritual essence and its prophetic powers for our times, and reinterpret all former art on the background of this experience. In this, artists as well as managers and politicians fo cultural affairs have to muster the courage to be unpopular, and have to finally stop looking fixedly at the media mechanisms with their sales quotas, numbers of viewers and listeners, and public relations successes. A star-studded gala event that eats up just as much money as the annual budget of an ensemble devoting itself to modern music out of idealism, such an event is unjustifiable not only from an artistic viewpoint, but rather from a political one. I personally experienced (in Hamburg) that some politicians are incapable of understanding the connection, and consider themselves progressive when they make up for "galas" by providing some funds for street music or so-called neighborhood culture. Politicians must help the right people, and must stress what is right rather than, by means of cheap and easy successes, keeping superficial mechanisms going. Mortier in Salzburg will be a test case. As long as the public views the Modern as an elitist game, it is kept from unfolding its moral, thereby explicitly "political" strength within society.

Shortly before his death, Luigi Nono gave some clues as to how we can gain a new understanding of our course as musicians even in a very chaotic society, and his words may serve as closing remarks to this sketch: "Rejection of the dogmas of fixed model—creating human needs—taking risks—creating a different, new way of listening in order to invent new feelings—awakening the ear, the eyes, the human brain, it's intelligence; the maximum of externally directed internalization is crucial today."

Translated by Sabine Tober

·21·

ON LOSS

GÜNTER GRASS

In the summer, my wife and I visited the small Danish island of Møn. We have been going there for years and by now have learned that to travel such a small distance offers no real escape from the news, particularly in the crisis month of August. The previous year the attempted coup in the disintegrating Soviet Union kept us huddled round the radio; the year before it was blanket coverage of the Gulf crisis; this year it was Germany.

The island of Møn has plenty to offer. It is a stopping-off place for a thousand and more gray geese, and in August there is heavy air traffic on the wide grazing pastures sheltered by Baltic dunes. All day long the geese practice take-off and landing. Sometimes herons will suddenly plunge and scatter them: wild consternation that gradually abates. The sky above the dunes and sea is always full of their formations.

Last August, though, the sky was empty but for a few seagulls. The dry summer had parched the grazing grounds, and there were no geese on the great airfields. Only the crises still arrived punctually by wireless. Two events arrived together, the sporting successes and failures of Barcelona and the war in Bosnia. The news overlapped. Events happening at the same time became the same events. The Olympic Games were being held in Sarajevo; the stadium was within reach of Serbian artillery. Here they totted up medals, there it was casualties. Terror became an Olympic discipline. A younger writer than me, with a lighter touch, would have found words to cover both arenas in one epic narrative: snipers and Ladies' Epée, beta blockers and blockade runners, abridged national anthems and the seventeenth pointless ceasefire, one lot of fireworks here, another there. . . .

But all I noted down were thoughts about Germany. My confounded leaden-footedness! On our gray-goose island, we tried to avoid the disruptions of the crisis month; after all, blackberries abounded and there was fresh fish every day. But even between the chopped-off flounder heads—wrapped in yesterday's newspaper—there was room for small print and scraps of headlines.

What is it that desensitizes sensitive people? We were irritable, but also dulled. Too much was happening at once. Can we blame the surfeit of information for our apathetic society: one person stares at the hole in the ozone layer, another harps on about the cost of health insurance. Spend too long wailing about the misery of the Bosnian refugees, and you forget to think about Somalia where people starve every day. Is the world out of joint or is it only the stock market going crazy again?

When the Games were over, Sarajevo had the headlines all to itself for a while, until even that nightmare no longer frightened us. Then came news from Germany, and we knew it was truly August.

In a way, it was nothing new, just the old story again. Over five hundred right-wing extremists repeatedly stormed a refugee hostel in Rostock-Lichtenhagen. From nearby windows, the citizenry looked on and applauded as stones and Molotov cocktails hit their targets. The police respected the display of popular will and kept well back. Shortly afterwards, they enthusiastically set off to arrest left-wing counterdemonstrators: to avoid possible escalation, as they said. On our radio we heard the politicians vying with one another in their well-rehearsed expressions of dismay.

But then more and more people watched the refugee hostels burning. The chanting was filmed and syndicated abroad. The "ugly face of Germany" was rediscovered. There were no distractions this time, not the Olympics, not Kabul, not Sarajevo. ROSTOCK it said in big letters wherever you looked. And on my holiday island in Denmark—a country not overly fond of foreigners, but a place where recourse to the murderous hatred of Rostock is barely imaginable—I jotted down some questions: Is there no end to German recidivism? Do Germans necessarily botch everything, even the unification that was handed to us on a plate? Are we condemned to relive our history? Are we, even now, incapable of humane treatment of one another? What do we lack, with all our wealth?

Since Rostock, Germany has changed. We now know that all the assurances of those unification-happy days were hollow. The newspapers trumpeted the end of the postwar era, the beginning of a new chapter in our history—a dozen eager historians stood by to write it. But now all the repugnant triumphalist din has stopped, and the past has tapped us on the shoulder.

Not that the shock of being collared silenced us quite. There have been protests, demonstrations to prove our capacity to fight back; but the politics responsible for our lapse into barbarism over the last three years have remained on course: the individual right to asylum—the jewel of our Constitution!—continues to be sacrificed to the god of popular feeling; the process of unification without unity accelerates; and neither government nor opposition is willing or able to call a halt to the shameless auctioning-off of the bankrupt GDR and think about how the burden might be shared.

The unfairness of that apportioning of the load has repeatedly driven me to speak out. For forty years the second-class citizens of the GDR, exploited, walled in, spied on, and spoken for, have had to pay for the war on behalf of the whole of Germany. Bad luck they did not make it to the west and freedom. Rather than acknowledging our debt, we in the west gave them more big-brothering. On December 18, 1989, at the Social Democrats' Party Congress in Berlin, I called for "a complete program of burden-sharing, to begin immediately and without further preconditions." It should, I suggested, be financed out of arms cuts and a special graded income tax; but my comrades still preferred to believe in Willy Brandt's attractive phrase, "what belongs together will grow together," even though it was clear, not many weeks after the collapse of the Wall, that not a lot was growing except a great many undesirable weeds. After forty years apart, all that we Germans have in common is the burden of a guilty past; even our language now divides us.

My speech about burden sharing was quickly buried under a perfunctory round of applause. Since then, I have been a voice in the wilderness. On February 2, 1990, at a conference in Tutzing addressing "New Answers to the German Question," I argued that "Whoever thinks about Germany now, and seeks answers for the German question, must include Auschwitz in his thoughts."

That sentence, and further reflections of mine, warning against an over-hasty German unification and proposing a confederal structure for the two states, provoked a furor. I, the "self-proclaimed gloom merchant of the nation" and "notorious enemy of Germany unity," had, I was told, tried to use Auschwitz to restrict the German right to self-determination.

I should like to know if my unification-drunk critics of the time thought the same when the so-called Jewish barracks in Sachsenhausen were burned to the ground? Or now that gypsies—nearly half a million Romany and Sinti people were murdered at Auschwitz and Auschwitz-Birkenau—are once again subjected to violence in Germany? Those critics—all of them parroting the silly stationmaster's line, "The train has left the station"—should have considered where their metaphorical train would terminate.

The time for warnings is long past. And yet still there is no political force willing or able to prevent this new wave of crimes. Far from it: it was not the skinheads who first broke the democratic consensus. The recent agreement by Interior Minister Seiters with the Romanian government that provides for the repatriation of gypsies, and the stream of attacks on the asylum article in the Constitution, are merely more elaborate versions of the slogan that presently unites all Germany: "Foreigners out!"

The Federal Republic and its constitution have been handed over to the tender mercies of a demolition company. When a Christian Democratic politician, a finance minister no less, ventures a look into the future from under his shaggy brows and proclaims that future elections can only be won right of center; when the Free Democrats borrow a brownish-shirted populist Austrian to address their meetings; when the minister representing the arms lobby proposes to go to Peenemünde to celebrate the golden anniversary of the V-2 rocket—and it takes protests from abroad to dissuade him; and when this whole slide to the right is dismissed as barroom chatter—then it is time we Germans recognized the threat we pose once more, preferably before our neighbors do.

As I mentioned, in this hard, dry summer, the geese had stopped flying to our holiday island. I had no distractions. The bitter lees of two years of unity finally leaked out onto paper. My Danish notes insist that I speak personally, of Germany and myself. How I did not want to let go of the country. How it slipped from my grasp. What I miss. What I do not. My *losses*.

I noted a long line of losses, which I will cut to a few representative examples. The first of them is the loss of my homeland. But that loss, painful though it was, was also justified. German culpability for the criminal conduct of the war, the genocide of Jews and gypsies, the murder of millions of prisoners of war and forced laborers, the crime of euthanasia, the sufferings we brought to our neighbors, especially the Polish people, when we occupied their countries, all that led to the loss of my homeland.

Compared to millions of refugees faced with the difficulties of settling in the West, I had a relatively easy time of it. Language did not compensate me for my loss, but by stringing words together I was able to make something in which my loss could be declared.

Most of my books invoke the old city of Danzig, its flat and hilly surroundings and the dull pulse of the Baltic; and with the years, Gdansk, too, has become a subject for me. Loss has given me a voice. Only what is entirely lost demands to be endlessly named: there is a mania to call the lost thing until it returns. Without loss there would be no literature. (I could almost market that as a thesis.)

Furthermore, the loss of my homeland has offered me the opportunity of new loyalties. If you have a home, you tend to want to stay in it; but I am curious about the world and take delight in traveling. People without a homeland have broader horizons than those who live where their fathers and forefathers did. I needed no crutch of nationalism to feel myself to be German: I had my loss.

Other values became important to me. Their loss is harder to bear because the gaps they left cannot be filled. I am used to being controversial in what I write and say, but in the last three years—the length of time I have been critical of the bungled process of unification and warned of its mindless speed—I have been forced to realize that I have been writing and speaking in a vacuum. My own loyalty, not to the state but to its constitution, was unwanted.

I freely admit that this sense of talking in a vacuum is a new experience for me, and not one I particularly enjoy. Was it ever different? Yes! For a few years, when Willy Brandt was chancellor, and tried to put the program of his government—"Dare to be more democratic!"—into effect. For Willy Brandt, contact with intellectuals was an essential stimulant: when still mayor of Berlin, he and his wife Ruth hosted discussions that were critical and frank and shattered a few Berliner illusions. "Political culture" is a hollow phrase nowadays, but for a time then it meant something and we listened to one another—another one of Willy Brandt's virtues.

When the writer Siegfried Lenz and I accompanied him as chancellor to Warsaw in 1970, we felt we had more than an ornamental function: because Lenz and I had both accepted the loss of our homeland, we brought with us recognition of Poland's western borders. Were we proud of Germany then? Yes, looking back I am proud to have been with that party in Warsaw. But as I try to remember that brief, important time, I realize I am talking about a lost era. With his death, Willy Brandt made the loss still clearer to me.

More losses: what happened to diversity of opinion? Nowadays the editorial lines of the papers are indistinguishable; they save their trivial disagreements for coy subclauses. The huffy dismissal of the democratic left is part of the bon ton today. One Fatherland, one feuilleton.

Also in the list of losses I would cite the Bundestag's decision to transfer the capital from Bonn to Berlin, and the tacit overturning of this decision by current Bonn practice. It is a circus in which the President of the Bundestag is the ringmaster, and the media are performers. The expensive hall for future debates has been inaugurated. But everything else goes on as before. Meanwhile, east of the Elbe, the child has fallen into the well.

The child has fallen into the well, and it is screaming. What is it screaming? It is screaming for *more*. People here in the west avert their ears. Have we Germans become so alienated from one another that all we care about are our own petty interests and possessions? And could it be that the coolness between Germans has produced the current, disgraceful xenophobia directed against those other strangers whom we call foreigners?

I walked off my rage about Rostock on the Danish holiday island; later I tried to etch it into copper plates with a cold needle: scratching as therapy.

But when my rage cooled, sadness and anger still remained. And accordingly, my notes demanded: What have you done to my country? How did this failed union come about? What madness prompted the electorate to entrust this difficult and politically demanding task to a fat figure masseur? What slick director turned our disunited land into a subject for talk shows? What dull-wittedness got us to pile the injustices of our capitalist system on top of those of "real socialism"? What's the matter with us?

Perhaps we lack the very people we are afraid of, because they are foreign to us and look foreign. Those whom, out of fear, we meet with hatred, which now daily turns to violence. And perhaps those we most lack are the ones we think of as the lowest of the low, the Romanies and the Sinti, the gypsies.

They have no allies. No politician represents their case, whether in the European Parliament or the Bundestag. No state they can appeal to would support their demands for compensation—pathetic, is it not?—for Auschwitz, or make them a national priority.

The Romanies and Sinti are the lowest of the low. "Expel them!" says Herr Seiters and gets on the line to Romania. "Smoke them out!" shout the skinheads. But in Romania and everywhere else, gypsies are bottom of the heap as well. Why?

Because they are different. Because they steal, are restless, roam, have the Evil Eye and that stunning beauty that makes us ugly to ourselves. Because their mere existence puts our values into question. Because they are all very well in operas and operettas, but in reality—it sounds awful, reminds you of awfulness—they are antisocial, odd and do not fit in. "Torch them!" shout the skinheads.

When Heinrich Böll was laid to rest seven years ago, there was a gypsy band leading the pallbearers—Lev Kopelev, Günter Wallraff, myself and Böll's sons, and the mourners on the way to the graveyard. It was Böll's wish. It was what he wanted to play him into the grave, that deeply tragic, despairingly gay music. It has taken me until now to understand him.

Let half a million and more Sinti and Romanies live among us. We need them. They could help us by irritating our rigid order a little. Something of their way of life could rub off on us. They could teach us how meaningless frontiers are: careless of boundaries, Romanies and Sinti are at home all over Europe. They are what we claim to be: born Europeans!

Translated by Michael Hofmann

AFTERWORD

VOLKMAR SANDER

The essays collected here were originally published in Germany in December 1992 and were edited by Wilhelm von Sternburg under the title *For a Civil Republic: Views on the Threatened Democracy in Germany.* They constituted the first alarmed outcry of a wide spectrum of concerned citizens against the murderous violence, neo-Nazi radicalism, and xenophobia that had raised grave doubts about the ability of the newly united Germany to cope with its problems. Of its original forty-two contributions, twenty-one are reprinted here, followed by the speech by Günter Grass, which this impassioned proponent of decency and human rights had delivered in Munich on November 18, 1992, and dedicated to the three Turkish women who had been murdered in Mölln earlier that year. Parallel to these rather spontaneous and personal expressions of outrage there appeared an urgent *Manifesto,* edited by Marion Countess Dönhoff, the editor of the weekly *Die Zeit,* and signed by several prominent figures from politics and industry, including the former chancellor Helmut Schmidt and Edzard Reuter, chairman of the board of Daimler-Benz. This forceful manifesto was followed by a lengthy and sober analysis of the political as well as economic reasons why; thus its subtitle "the country must change." It has remained on the German best-seller list ever since. Whereas Sternburg's and Grass's appeal were directed to the public at large, the manifesto by Dönhoff et. al. focused more on the failed politics of the present Bonn government. Taken together, however, they had a powerful influence and served as a necessary reminder to an all-too-complacent audience that, political and economic muscle notwithstanding, a community is only as strong as the care and respect it gives its weakest members, and that indeed there was a real political and moral crisis.

In 1992, right-wing extremists committed over two-thousand acts of violence in Germany, ninety percent of them directed against foreigners. When compared to other European countries, actually this number is not unusually high. According to a Congressional Research Service Report to Congress (March 29, 1993, p. 3), Germany's total of 4,587 "criminal acts against foreigners" in 1992 compared with 7,780 "racially motivated attacks" in Britain, and similar figures for Sweden, France, Italy, and Spain. What makes Germany's case so exceptional and alarming is both the dramatic increase over the short span of only two years and the fact that so much of the violence is carried out by right-wing extremists. Even when no physical violence is involved, the all-pervasive slogans of "Foreigners Out," "Germany to the Germans," and anti-Semitic slurs are hauntingly familiar and understandably have raised fears of a relapse into a tragic past.

In the volatile atmosphere of present-day politics in Germany, a great deal has happened since the contributions in this book were written last fall. Although the central problems remain, much also has changed, and the voices gathered here fortunately no longer are the exception. The public's initial shock and stunned apathy by and large have been overcome and replaced by political activism on all levels. Official statements are forthcoming, belatedly but forcefully now, from President Richard von Weizsäcker to foundations, academics, news media, and the public itself. Public spokesmen of virtually all the nation's prestigious organizations have gone on record denouncing political extremism and pleading for tolerance. A strongly worded "Appeal Against Hatred of Foreigners" was signed by the chairman of the Science Council, and the respective presidents of the Humboldt Foundation, the Max Planck Society, the German Research Association, the Conference of University Rectors, and others. Laws already on the books but traditionally fully activated only against left-wing extremists are now being used against the right as well; new laws have been passed; several neo-Nazi groups have been banned altogether.

Most impressive, however, if only for its sheer numbers, was the spectacle of an aroused public taking to the streets, and demonstrating its opposition in *Lichterketten* (candlelight vigils) that stretched for miles. Starting in Munich, but quickly spilling over to Hamburg, Berlin, and other cities, people turned out by the hundreds of thousands to show their solidarity. Stephen Kinzer's headline in the *New York Times* (January 13, 1993) was "Germany Ablaze: It's Candlelight, Not Firebombs." By February 1993 it was estimated that their total number had surpassed the three-million mark. A rock concert in Frankfurt, with 150,000 in attendance and hundreds of millions more worldwide watching through live television coverage, rallied their fans under the motto *Heute sie—Morgen du* (Them today—You tomorrow). Major-league soccer events followed, their industrial sponsors foregoing their rights to have team players display their logo so they could wear slogans such as "My friend is a foreigner." It turned into a massive movement, almost to the point of becoming a German version of political correctness, making it chic to be against xenophobia. And it changed the mood of the country, or so it seemed.

Immigration in virtually all industrialized states is running at historically high levels. During the late seventies, Jean-Marie Le Pen founded the National Front around the slogan "France for the French," drawing eventually almost 14 percent of the vote nationwide. This in turn caused other politicians to join what they perceived as a winning cause. Mitterand said immigration had passed "the threshold of tolerance"; other mainstream politicians warned of an immigrant "invasion," thereby making it respectable to be anti-immigrant, which this year finally resulted in a tightening of France's hitherto liberal immigration laws. Le Pen's tactic was imitated by Jörg Haider in Austria and echoed by Franz Schönhuber, a former SS officer and leader of the right-wing Republicans in Germany, with similar success. Haider's FPÖ, Austria's nominally liberal but in fact right-wing populist party, is drawing about 20 percent of the vote, making it that country's third largest party. Schönhuber's Republicans stunned the political establishment by receiving more than eight percent of the vote in local elections held on March 7, 1993, in the western state of Hesse, which strongly indicated that they will be represented in the Federal Parliament next year. Most certainly they will be represented in many more local governments as a result of the other eighteen elections scheduled for 1994 throughout Germany, including local elections in the five eastern states, their first since unification. The current prospect is that this extreme-right fringe in all three countries may prove to be a permanent feature of European politics.

Although unchecked immigration poses obvious problems even to the richest countries, deteriorating economic conditions are exacerbating ethnic conflicts even more. The dawning age of economic migration and rising racism is changing not just images but politics everywhere. In the case of Germany the issue is further complicated by confusing the distinction between immigration and asylum. Most observers now agree that Germany's immigration laws were too restrictive, whereas its laws concerning asylum-seekers were too liberal.

Bonn's asylum law is based on Article 16 of the Constitution, which simply states: "Persons persecuted on political grounds shall enjoy the right of asylum." It is a unique law, born out of shame for the past and gratitude for the help afforded by other countries to the 800,000, mostly political dissidents and Jews, who fled Hitler's Reich, and Germans of all parties were at one time proud of it as an emblem of moral rebirth. But the law was meant to provide refuge against political persecution, not as an open invitation for people suffering from economic hardships.

By not clearly making this distinction, many German politicians, especially on the right, actively encouraged xenophobia purely for party gains years before the current crisis, which was thus long in coming. When the numbers suddenly swelled disproportionately after the collapse of the old equilibrium, the opening of long-sealed borders and the outbreak of ethnic wars, violence ensued. In 1991, sixty percent of all asylum-seekers who arrived in western Europe went to Germany; France and Britain each took in thirteen percent. Germany, already more densely populated than most countries, thus accepted more refugees than all other European countries combined. Last year's figure was 438,191, up from 256,112 in 1991 and 193,063 in 1990. A total of 118,064 persons applied for asylum in Germany in the first three months of 1993 (*German Information Center,* May 14, 1993). In addition to official asylum-seekers, there is a large number of "illegal" refugees. Germany shares a porous 800-mile-long border with Poland and the Czech Republic, which is difficult to police and leaves the country open to immigration from Central and Eastern Europe, as well as the former Soviet Union. Official estimates put the figure of people who entered Germany illegally in this way at 310,000 in 1992 alone (*Congressional Research Service,* March 29, 1993 p. 17).

In a speech on October 3, 1992, marking the Day of German Unity, President von Weizsäcker urgently appealed to politicians of all parties to abandon their jockeying to gain tactical advantages and to join in a serious discussion of the issue in a national debate for legal reforms.

Clearly, the mounting pressure of public resentment made more stringent enforcement a practical necessity. Several bilateral treaties were negotiated. Since more than half of the foreigners asking for asylum came from Romania and Bulgaria, most of them Gypsies, the first of these was signed with Romania. It was followed by a treaty with Poland in May of this year, and negotiations for a similar accord with the Czech Republic are under way. The German–Polish agreement is supposed to have "model character," providing stricter border controls and eventually allowing the Germans to deport rejected applicants within six months of their arrival from Poland. Since, according to Interior Minister Seiters, it was "not Germany's intent to shove the asylum-seeker problem onto other countries," Germany will pay Poland about 150-million dollars over two years to help with providing shelter for the rejected immigrants.

By far the most important reform, however, dealt with Article 16 of the Constitution. For fifteen years, ever since 1978, ten efforts by Parliament to change the asylum law had failed. Now under mounting pressure from all sides, not least the general public, and fearful of the 1994 general elections, the opposition Social Democratic Party agreed to amend the law. Its support was vital, since a new constitutional amendment required a two-thirds majority in Parliament. The amendment was passed by huge margins in May 1993 (521 to 132 in the *Bundestag;* 12 to 4 in the *Bundesrat*).

The main reason to support the change was the argument that 95 percent of those refugees asking for asylum in recent years were not fleeing political persecution but trying to immigrate for economic reasons. Seeking jobs rather than refuge was not considered appropriate under Article 16. So under the new law prospective refugees are separated according to their country of origin. Any refugee coming from a country that Germany considers free of persecution will immediately be sent home. Others, like the five percent last year ultimately found to be truly political refugees, will still be admitted under the old law.

While the new law was being passed, 10,000 protesters demonstrated outside the Bundestag in Bonn. Others sadly commented that the change, overdue for years, had been brought about only under pressure from neo-Nazi thugs and that it looked as if they could now claim a political victory. A *New York Times* editorial stated that "having set so liberal an example, Germany has bowed to circumstances that can only cause sorrow even among those who strive to sympathize." (May 31, 1993). Yet it seems only fair to point out that the constitutional guarantee of asylum, a law that does not even exist anywhere else in the world, was not abolished but merely amended to prevent its abuse. Refugees from the fighting in the Balkans are still being admitted.

The political and intellectual elite in Germany, hitherto quite accustomed to moralizing and exhorting others, was shocked to learn that in 1992, for the first time, their country had been included in the Human Rights Helsinki Watch List. That highly acclaimed international forum, actively supported in its fact-finding by German sources, including the Democratic Socialist Party and the Green Party, had found that "responsibility for the police failure ultimately rests with the highest levels of state and federal government. Germany has the economic resources, it has the technology and know-how to respond to violent outbreaks such as the one in Rostock. What appears to be lacking is the political will." (Helsinki Watch, *Foreigners Out,* October 1992, p. 39)

As mentioned before, this earlier denial is slowly being replaced by increased focus on political action. With more time and reflection, however, the realization is also dawning that apart from the formidable problems of violence there are other roots particular to the German situation. During its 40 years, the old Federal Republic had actually not done badly in integrating some four-and-a-half million foreigners, roughly seven percent of the population. But those were prosperous times when "guest workers" were not only welcome: without them the "economic miracle" would have been slower in coming if not stopped completely. Now the skyrocketing influx of foreigners competing for jobs in a depressed market economy is felt to be doubly threatening. Large groups of people are unemployed, particularly in the former GDR, where whole industries were shut down, but also in the Ruhr district in the West, where the steel industry has again fallen on hard times. In the East, even workers who are still holding on to a precarious job for the moment are afraid that in the long run they will be superfluous, and that there is no place for them in the new Germany. Suffering from multiple dislocations and disappointments, and coming from relatively secure surroundings (albeit rather frugal and politically unfree), they have fallen into a vacuum in which all the certainties that had shaped their lives have vanished. After the early euphoria had worn off, West Germans in turn were slow in understanding the full psychological and economic impact of unity. Only when the flames of Rostock were beamed round the world did they realize that suddenly, and irreversibly, they had in fact gained not just half a million but sixteen-million economic refugees, and that they were about to change their country.

Consequently, during the early months of this year the targets of rage and frustration seem to have shifted somewhat. The shock value of attacking asylum-seekers and desecrating Jewish cemeteries has diminished: the new scapegoats to be zeroed in on are the politicians. Germans are upset by the seeming inability of politicians in Bonn to deal with the problems, and repelled by their opportunistic behavior. A new word is making the rounds: *Politikverdrossenheit,* denoting frustration with all things political. That attitude has already influenced voting patterns, not only by attracting protest votes to the right-wing Republicans but also making nonvoters the largest group of all. This is a common phenomenon elsewhere, but it is the first time it has happened in postwar Germany, and has come as a shock to many.

Some observers, fearful that a haunting past may repeat itself, are asking "What Rough Beast is Reborn" (Norman Birnbaum, *The Nation,* April 5, 1993). Others cautiously hope that just because of the past, Germany of all the countries in a world with neo-Nazi stirrings might be the least likely to succumb again. The verdict is not yet in, and certainly postwar Germany has never been tested by an economic problem on this scale. Yet, it has all happened before. The thirteen million refugees from the east, which West Germany absorbed immediately after World War II, came under very different circumstances. Still, full integration might and probably will happen again in time. If compared to the problems of Prague, Warsaw, Kiev, and points further east, even the very real present problems of Leipzig or East Berlin seem trivial.

What is the future of German Democracy? The sad, alarmed, concerned voices gathered here are an indication of the dangers threatening it and the urgency to defend it. Günter Grass's speech on loss also describes the decline of political culture and the deterioration of civil discourse. The danger signals are obvious and must be taken seriously. Yet most observers still agree that Bonn is not Weimar, that in sharp contrast to the period preceding Hitler's rise to power, the Bonn Republic for the past forty-four years has been a model of political, social, and economic stability. That too, after all, is part of Germany's history. In addition, Germany has also become deeply integrated into the European Community. But most important of all, Germany's problems are not Germany's alone. The imminent and worldwide problem of economic migration will be solved, if it *can* be solved, only in concert with other nations.

For people old enough to remember, there is some sort of twisted irony here, not mentioned by any of the contributors to this book. The last time the world looked on in horror Jews, political opponents, and other decent people desperately wanted to get out of Germany. This time people desperately want to get in. Of course there is no comparing the two periods, but it is a grim reminder of what grotesque tricks history can play.

In the meantime it is to be hoped that ways may be found to end the divisions and the hatred that disfigure this country, as they do so many others. The millions of German citizens who marched in candlelight protests to express the national sense of revulsion over the violence were as encouraging as the individual opinions of outrage expressed in this book.

Similar expressions continue today. But so does the violence.

THE CONTRIBUTORS

WALTER BOEHLICH, born in 1921, writer, essayist, cultural philosopher. Living in Frankfurt am Main.

SILVIA BOVENSCHEN, born 1946, teaches German literature at the University of Frankfurt am Main. Her text was written for broadcast by Bayerischer Rundfunk (Radio Bavaria).

DANIEL COHN-BENDIT, born 1945, was one of the leaders of the French student movement; journalist and author; currently city commissioner for multicultural affairs, Frankfurt am Main. His most recent book (with Thomas Schmidt) is *Heimat Babylon. Das Wagnis der multikulturellen Demokratie* (The hazardous enterprise of multicultural democracy) (Babylon, Native Place).

FRIEDRICH DIECKMANN, born 1937 in Landsberg/Werthe, now Poland, grew up in Dresden, author. His last book was *Vom Einbringen/ Väterländische Beiträge* (*On participating/patriotic contributions*). Living in Berlin.

FREIMUT DUVE, born 1936, politician, author and editor, member of the Bundestag (Social Democrats) from Hamburg since 1979.

ERNST ERLITZ, born 1941, television journalist, author of TV documentaries and moderator of popular series *(Kennzeichen; Pro und Contra);* currently editor-in-chief of Süddeutscher Rundfunk (Radio Stuttgart). Last book: *Sie waren dabei: Ost-deutsche Profile von Bärbel-Boley zu Lothar de Maiziere* (They were part of it: East German profiles).

PETER ESCHBERG, born 1936, Director of Municipal Theater, Frankfurt am Main.

HEINER GEISSLER, born 1930, politician. Member of the Bundestag since 1956, prominent leader of the Christian Democratic Party, general secretary from 1977 to 1989. Minister in various cabinets; most recently: secretary of youth, family, and health in Bonn 1982–85.

RALPH GIORDANO, born 1923, television journalist and writer; author of more than one hundred documentary films, among them the largely autobiographical four-part television version of his novel *Die Bertinis* (1988). Last publication: *Ich bin angenagelt an dieses Land. Reden und Aufsätze über die deutsche Vergangenheit und Gegenwart* (I am nailed down to this country. Speeches and essays on Germany past and present) 1992.

GÜNTER GRASS, born 1927 in Danzig, (now Gdansk/Poland), writer. The speech printed here was delivered on November 18, 1992 at the Munich *Kammerspiel* Theater, and dedicated to the memory of Yeliz Anslan, Ayshe Yilmaz, and Bahide Arslan, the three Turkish women murdered in Mölln last year.

ALFRED GROSSER, born 1925, in Frankfurt am Main, emigrated to France in 1933. Professor of German and political science in Paris, Friedenspreis des deutschen Buchhandels 1975. Numerous lectures, TV appearances, and publications on politics, particularly French-German relations. His latest book is *Mein Deutschland* (My Germany), 1993.

PETER HÄRTLING, born 1933 in Chemnitz, in West Germany since 1946; writer of poetry, fiction, plays; received many prizes; living near Frankfurt am Main.

ROBERT GERALD LIVINGSTON, born 1927, retired US diplomat, founder and director of the American Institute for Contemporary German Studies, an affiliate of Johns Hopkins University.

PETER VON OERTZEM, born 1924, taught political science at the University of Hannover, prominent leader of the Social Democratic Party, minister of culture (Lower Saxony 1970–74), numerous publications.

FRITZ PLEITGEN, born 1938, journalist. For many years bureau chief for ARD (First German Television) in Washington, East Berlin, Moscow. Currently television editor-in-chief of WDR (West German Radio and TV) in Cologne.

LEA ROSH, born 1936, print and TV journalist. Last publication: *Der Tod ist ein Meister aus Deutschland. Deportationen und Ermordung der Juden. Kollaboration und Verweigerungin Europa* (Death is a master from Germany: Deportation and murder of the Jews. Collaboration and denial).

VOLKMAR SANDER, born 1929, Erich Maria Remarque Professor of German and director of Deutsches Haus at New York University.

KLAUS SCHLESINGER, born 1937, writer of poetry and fiction; in the GDR until 1980, now living in (West) Berlin.

THOMAS SCHMID, born 1945, writer. Last publication (with Daniel Cohn-Bendit, q.v.) *Heimat Babylon.* Living in Frankfurt am Main.

HELMUT SCHMIDT, born 1918, German Chancellor, 1974–82; co-publisher of *Die Zeit,* Hamburg. Last publication *Handeln für Deutschland* (To act for Germany), 1993. The text printed here is taken from a speech delivered on October 3, 1992, at the Paulskirche in Frankfurt am Main.

WILHELM VON STERNBURG, born 1939, journalist and writer. Television editor-in-chief, Radio Hesse, Frankfurt/M. Last book publication (with E. Jäckel) *Fall und Aufstieg der deutschen Nation. Nachdenken über einen Massenrausch* (Fall and rise of the German nation. Thoughts about mass hysteria), 1993.

WOLFGANG THIERSE, born 1943, in Breslau (now Wroclaw, Poland). Worked in the Central Institute for Literary History in (East) Berlin. Since January, 1990 member of the newly reconstituted Social Democratic Party, since June 1990 as its chairman. As a result of the first all-German elections in December 1990, he was elected member of the Bundestag. He is also vice chairman of the SPD.

HEINRICH AUGUST WINKLER, born 1938 in Königsberg (now Kaliningrad/Russia), professor of history. Most recent publication: *Arbeiter und Arbeiterbewegung in der Geschichte der Weimarer Republik 1918–38* (Workers and the labor movement in the Weimar Republic 1918–38). 3 volumes. Living in Berlin.

HANS ZENDER, born 1936, composer, conductor, and university professor. Living near Frankfurt am Main.